Chance or the Dance?

THOMAS HOWARD

Chance or the Dance?

A Critique of Modern Secularism

Ignatius Press   San Francisco

Previous edition published by
Harold Shaw Publishers
Wheaton, Illinois
© 1969 Thomas T. Howard

Cover by Marcia Ryan

ISBN 0-89870-229-1
Library of Congress catalogue number 88-83750
Printed in the United States of America

For Professor Kilby
who took my arm and said, "*Look*"

Contents

Acknowledgments

While there are no footnotes in the following pages, it will be perfectly obvious to many readers that a hundred acknowledgments are due to Charles Williams, J. R. R. Tolkien, C. S. Lewis, and T. S. Eliot. If there is anything here which makes sense, it probably derives from something which one or another of these gentlemen has said somewhere. Any woolly-mindedness and bad workmanship are mine.

Is it chance
or dance moves
the world?

Is the world
blind and dumb
or bloom, festal?
A vain jest,
or holy feast?

Eugene Warren,
"Christographia XIV"

Chapter One

The Old Myth and the New

There were some ages in Western history that have occasionally been called Dark. They were dark, it is said, because in them learning declined, and progress paused, and men labored under the pall of *belief.* A cause-effect relationship is frequently felt to exist between the pause and the belief. Men believed in things like the Last Judgment and fiery torment. They believed that demented people had devils in them, and that disease was a plague from heaven. They believed that they had souls, and that what they did in this life had some bearing on the way in which they would finally experience reality. They believed in portents and charms and talismans. And they believed that God was in heaven and Beelzebub in hell and that the Holy Ghost had impregnated the Virgin Mary and that the earth and sky were full of angelic and demonic conflict. Altogether, life was very weighty, and there was no telling what might lie behind things. The ages were, as I say, dark.

Then the light came. It was the light that has lighted us men into a new age. Charms, angels, devils, plagues, and parthenogenesis have fled from the glare into the crannies of memory. In their place have come coal mining and $E = mc^2$ and plastic and group dynamics and napalm and urban renewal and rapid transit. Men were freed from the fear of the Last Judgment; it was felt to be more bracing to face Nothing than to face the Tribunal. They were freed from worry about getting their souls into God's heaven by the discovery that they had no souls and that God had no heaven. They were freed from the terror of devils and plagues by the knowledge that the thing that was making them scream and foam was not an imp but only their own inability to cope, and that the thing that was clawing out their entrails was not divine wrath but only cancer. Altogether, life became much more livable since it was clear that in fact nothing lay behind things. The age was called enlightened.

The myth sovereign in the old age was that everything means everything. The myth sovereign in the new is that nothing *means* anything.

That is, to the darkened mind it did not mean nothing that the sun went down and night came and the moon and stars appeared and then dawn and the sun and morning again and another day, which would itself wax and then wane into twilight and dusk and night. It did not mean nothing to them that the time of work was under the aegis of the bright sun and that it was the sun that poured life into the seeds that they were planting and that brought out the sweat on their foreheads, and that the time of rest was under the scepter of the silver moon. This was the diurnal exhibition of what was True—that there are a panoply and a rhythm and a cycle, a waxing and a waning, a rising and a setting and then a rising again. And to them it was not for nothing that the king wore a crown of gold and that the lord mayor wore medallions. This was the political exhibition of what was, in fact, True—that there are royalty and authority and hierarchy at the heart of things and that it is possible to see this in lions and eagles and queen bees as well as in the court of the king. To them it was not for nothing that a man went in to a woman in private and uncovered her and knew ecstasy in the experience of her being. This was simply a case in point of what was True anyway—that there is a mystery of being not to be thrown open to all, and that the right knowledge of another being is ecstatic, and that what appears under these carnal forms is, in fact, the image of what is actually True.

The former mind, in a word, read vast significance into everything. Nature and politics and animals and sex—these were all exhibitions in their own way of the way things are. This mind fancied that everything meant everything, and that it all rushed up finally to heaven. We have an idea of royalty, this mind said, which we observe in our politics and which we attribute to lions and eagles, and we have this idea because there *is* a great King at the top of things, and he has set things thus so that our fancies will be drawn toward his royal Person, and we will recognize the hard realities of which the stuff of our world has been a poor shadow when we stumble into his royal court.

So this mind handled all the data of experience as though they were images—cases in point, that is, of each other and of the way things are. So that when they came across the idea, say, of the incarnation of the god, it made perfect sense to them, since it was in the nature of things to appear in images—royalty in lions and kings, strength in bulls and heroes, industriousness in ants and beavers, delicacy in butterflies and fawns, terror in oceans and thunder, glory in roses and sunsets—so of course the god might appear in flesh and blood, how else? And when they heard about a thing like resurrection, they could believe it, since they thought they could see the same thing (life issuing from death) in other realms—seedtime and harvest, and morning and evening, and renunciation and reward—and so what else did it all mean but that it is the way things are that life triumphs over death?

This mind saw things as images because it saw correspondences running in all directions among things. That is, the world was not a random tumble of things all appearing separately, jostling one another and struggling helter-skelter for a place in the sun. On the contrary, one thing signaled another. One thing was a case in point of another. A goshawk tearing a field mouse seemed a case in point of what is also visible in the fierce duke who plunders the neighboring duchy. A lamb was an instance of timidity, mildness, harmlessness. The earth receiving life from the sun and bringing forth grass and trees and nourishing everything from itself was like all the other mothers we can observe—doves and ewes and our own mothers. The inclination to trace correspondences among things transfigured those things—goshawks, lambs, the earth, kings— into images of one another, so that on all levels it was felt that *this* suggested *that*. It is a way of looking at things that goes farther than saying that this is *like* that: it says that *both this and that* are instances of the way things are. The sun pours energy into the earth and the man pours energy into the woman because that is how fruit begins—by the union of the one thing and the other; by the union of what appears under stellar categories as sun and earth, and under human categories as man and woman. That is, in both instances, there is enacted under the appropriate species what lies at the root of things.

Ironically, this way of looking at things did not die when the myth that made it possible died (the myth being that everything really does mean everything). When, under the fluorescent glare of the laboratory lights, the old myth died and the new myth (that nothing means anything) took over, men, without realizing what they were doing, kept on behaving and speaking of their experience *as though* everything meant everything. That is, their new myth told them that things are impersonal and abstract. They don't *mean* anything; they *are*. The method that led to the new myth was called the scientific method. It became sovereign when it was given the authority of dogma in the eighteenth century. The process was called Enlightenment, and it is the myth with which the modern world has supplanted the old myth.

But, oddly, the sovereignty of the new myth, ought to have slain the image-making inclination of man, since there is no reason at all to suppose, under the new, that one thing suggests another (lions suggesting kings who themselves suggest the King); no reason, that is, except fancy, for the laboratory has no equipment for chasing and tracing these orbiting and glorious correspondences in which the lion and the king appear as images; that is, as *serious* suggestions of something real). That sovereignty was like the sovereignty of the Roman emperor who insisted on being worshiped as a god. People obliged him but went on with their household gods anyway. The difference between them and us is that, whereas nobody supposed that he really *was* divine, we modern men *have* accepted the sovereignty of the new myth. We bow to the edict (Science is All) and then believe it. But, *all the while, all unaware, we keep the old myth alive.* It has trickled out of the old ages into the enlightened ages. It appears in a thousand ways, and in every case it belies the new myth. It is what makes us shake hands and set the table for lunch and say, "I felt like a fish out of water", and bring out cake and candles for a birthday and dance and write sonnets and go behind closed doors for sexual intercourse and stand up for a woman or the President and go to Mass. It is what makes us put on one dress for shopping and another for cocktails and another for the opera and another for church. It is what makes us put on beads and paisley and steel rims if we feel one way about society, and buttondown shirts and oxford cloth and plastic rims if we feel another way. For these things all suppose that one thing means another; that it is appropriate to make *this* (a handshake) say *this* ("Hello, I see you, I greet you", etc.); that one may signal in *this* realm (clothes) what is at work in *this* realm (political philosophy); that we may enact *thus* (sex behind closed doors) what is, in fact, true (that this knowledge of other beings is high and holy and not for the marketplace); that when we speak *this* way about some common thing (a sonnet about evening) we may be speaking more accurately than when we speak analytically, since the poetry is itself perhaps a case in point of something that is exhibited in the colors, tranquility, and clarity of the evening.

But these ways of doing things are all oddities. They do not fit the new myth. For where the old myth said, "This *indeed* means this, and eventually everything", the new says, "This *only* means this, and eventually nothing." The old myth traveled upward and outward; the new travels downward and inward. The old myth said, "I have a father, and this is to be expected since there is, in fact, a Father who has set things up so that I will have some way of grasping this notion of fatherness which is in the stuff of things. This [my father] *indeed* means this [*the* Father]." The new myth says, "You have projected your experience of your father onto the cosmos, so that the Father exists strictly as the extension of your own situation. This [*the* Father] *only* means this [your father]."

So that when a modern man acts as though there is a correspondence running among all things (whenever he uses a metaphor or simile, or any image, that is), he is saying, in effect, "Our inclinations fool us. But we won't be fooled. We know from scientific research that it is only imagination that leads us to project one thing onto another. To be sure, this is very often useful. It helps us communicate ideas. And it helps us cope with life. But it is just that—imagination—and nothing more. Things *look* as though they answer one to another, so we may speak of them in that way so long as we do not suppose that we are saying anything true thereby."

In other words, the faculty in us that establishes these correspondences among things, and hence allows us to see one thing as an image of another, is imagination, and the modern mind (the new myth) understands this to be a flight away from actuality. In this view, when primitive man spoke of the god of the wood, he was peopling an inanimate thing with projections of his own inclination to see things personal-istically. Similarly, when the Bible speaks of the fear of the *Lord* as the beginning of wisdom, this was a helpful, albeit fanciful, way of personalizing reality, so that an accurate modern rephrasing would be "A sense of modesty and awe when confronted by the phenomena of experience is appropriate." When Dante fancies hell and purgatory and heaven as real states of being, he is, of course, projecting the human experi-ence of alienation and discipline and bliss into a cosmic geography. When T. S. Eliot speaks of the journey of the Magi as a paradigm of human experience, we must remember that what the Magi found at Bethlehem was only an imaginary (that is, fanciful) thing and that there is no scientific (that is, serious) connection be-tween this and anything *real*.

Imagination, which is this faculty by which we sup-pose correspondences among all things and hence see them as images of one another (it is the *imag*ination— the image-making faculty), is understood in opposite ways by the old myth and the new: by the new it is seen as a flight into fancy; by the old it was seen pre-cisely as a flight toward actuality.

The new myth, I say, sees imagination as a flight into fancy—useful, to be sure, in helping us grasp rare abstractions like deity or ultimacy, or to articulate our experiences of grief or love or beauty, but undoubt-edly leading us astray to the extent that it makes us picture and personify things. After all, we know that mathematics and linguistic analysis and astrophysics are the disciplines under which we must describe our universe, and this whole mythopoeic way of speaking belongs to the ages that really believed that things

were all animated and charged with identity and being, all dancing in the great Dance. It was that sort of
thing that came up with the picture, for instance, of
God the Father as a bearded valetudinarian sitting on a
throne dressed in a golden cope and tri-regnum,
whereas our age knows that this is foolish and that no
such thing is the case. Insofar as we are prepared to
speak of "God" at all, we may say something about
the Ground of Being.

The argument of this book would applaud and de-
mur at both images. Of the old man on the throne, it
would say that if the image suggests wisdom and authority and majesty and antiquity and paternity and
personhood, good; if it suggests senility and pomp-
ousness, it has broken down. By exactly the same token, if the image of the Ground of Being suggests the
absolutely fundamental, the source, the foundation,
good; if it suggests abstraction and remoteness and
nonpersonhood, then it has broken down. Any image
gets botched.

The old myth, for its part, saw the image-making
faculty as a flight toward actuality. That is, it saw all
the data of experience precisely as epiphanies of what
was true at the heart of the matter, and felt that
therein lay their special validity. It would not, I suppose, have quarreled with the modern description of a
lion as such and such an organization of muscle,
blood, and bone. It would have been delighted and as-
tonished. But it would have been puzzled if we had
insisted, "That's all there is to it." What? But the lion
is the king of beasts! Look at the royal head! Look at
that regal pace! Beware its wrath! Of course it is what
you say it is—a complex of tissue and blood—and I

never would have found that out without your analytic method of inquiry into the lion's body. But
whatever makes you go on and say, "That's all there is
to it"? What a truncated view! What is your world
like, anyway, that you flatten it out this way? What *is*
this lion if he is not the epiphany of majesty? What are
eagles and kings all about? It's my fancy that makes
me speak thus? Oh, no—it's your own myopia and superstition that blind *you*.

In any case, there is the situation: the old myth saw
the world as image; the new sees it as a chance concat-
enation of physical events. This book is an attempt to
describe how our experience might look if we looked
at it once more under the terms of the old myth. Or,
put another way, to observe some of the regions in
which, probably unaware, we keep the old myth alive
by acting as though it were at least useful in organizing our experience. In the way we handle experience,
from ordinary conversation to social custom to poetry,
painting, ceremony, sex, and ritual, we do obeisance
to the old myth. Whether that obeisance is fanciful
and superstitious or is an authentic index of the way
things are is, of course, the big question. The modern
world supposes that it is the former. This book supposes that it is the latter. God (or somebody) will have
to let us know which is the case.

Chapter Two

Of Dishrags and Borzois

It is common enough for us to think of imagination as something for the poets, or, if it has anything to do with us, as brought into play only in our reveries when we dream of flying away to some fruited island in a tropical sea. But it is more than that. It is something that is at work in us every moment of our lives, sleeping and waking, and that shapes every thought we have about ourselves or anything else. Oh, very well, then, it is spice, it is garnishing, we may say. It adds a bit of flavor to the bland necessities of logical thought and the workaday worries that demand our attention so remorselessly.

It is, of course, possible to take this view of imagination. But to do so is to dismiss as parsley the entire mode under which we all think of experience. It is to say, in effect, that there is nothing of interest in a thing that is never for one moment dormant.

Imagination is a commonplace of our experience, and that is probably why we do not spend much time thinking about it, any more than we think about eyesight. We tread along from one year to the next, gladly accepting the rewards of eyesight, and it is not until we lose it that we have time to recognize that our whole experience of life was virtually determined by our ability to see—or at least that the nature of that experience must be drastically restructured now that things no longer exist for us in a visual mode.

But what is imagination, then, if it is more than reverie or fancy? Imagination is, in a word, the faculty by which we organize the content of our experience into some form, and thus apprehend it as significant. Put another way, it is what makes us refuse to accept experience as mere random clutter, and makes us try without ceasing to shape that experience so that we can manage it. We cannot live with the idea of mere randomness. All of us, besides merely *passing through* an experience (thirst, love, exhaustion), want to be able to *say something about* that experience. For if we can just get something said about it, we get a kind of detachment from it, and can savor it (in the case of a pleasant experience like love) or battle it (pain, say, or thirst). There comes, of course, a final point of intensity in any experience pushed to its extreme when we are past uttering anything at all and must succumb. For instance, although the experience of romantic love has aroused as much comment as anything in history, at the ultimate point of intensity in that experience (orgasm), words die away. Similarly, we may complain of thirst and our cries may become more and more shrill and agonized, but when the experience has reached its final intensity, we fall mute with caked and blackened tongues sticking to our dry lips. But, short of the silence that attends the final intensity of experience (ultimately the Beatific Vision or hell, presumably), there is this great paean of words and music and dancing and sculpting with which we greet experience. It is at work on all levels, from the child playing with his toy truck to our conversations over coffee to the noblest utterance of all, poetry.

How, then, does imagination appear in ordinary affairs? The most obvious way is in the expressions we use in conversation when we want to underline some idea. "Whew! I felt like a dishrag after that!" we gasp. It is doubtful that our skin felt like loosely knitted cloth to us, or that we felt soapy. What do we mean, then? We mean that we felt exhausted, and that it was all very taxing, and that if, for a moment, you can grant a comparison between a piece of cloth and a human being, our experience of the situation was, to us, what the dishrag's experience of being wrung out is. In other words, by calling upon some other area of familiar experience, we heighten our appreciation of the experience in question. The image of the dishrag says simply and immediately what a whole string of adjectives would have to try to say, and would say less effectively. By getting an *image* of what we mean from another realm of experience, we say exactly what we are trying to say.

Our conversation is full of this. Probably our high school English teacher, in the effort to get us to see that poetry is not so very far from common experience, led a class discussion asking for examples of the way we use metaphor (that is what this reaching out to other realms of experience for images is called) in daily conversation. We all joined in: "My face was red as a beet." "He had a voice like a foghorn." "He has guts." "He is a pompous ass." "You couldn't beat your way out of a paper bag." "This is a ticklish problem." "This is a dark day for America." "The hours dragged on." And so on. The teacher got his point across: we say scarcely anything without exercising this faculty. And when we do exercise it, it is in order to bring about a heightened awareness of the experience in question. To do so is to reach across a gulf that cannot be spanned ("a gulf that cannot be spanned"—how else shall I say it?) by the analytic faculty in us. There is little similarity between the dishrag and me. The one is small, flat, and square; the other is large, solid, and irregular; the one is cloth, the other flesh; the one is inanimate, the other animate; the one is passive, the other active. So that to draw upon one as in any way corresponding to the other is to engage in an absurdity. And yet we do it all the time; and it not only strikes us as not doing violence to things; it is positively helpful in heightening our awareness of experience.

If we look at imagination just on this level of ordinary conversation, we can see at least two things at work in it. In the first place, it is what might be called a synthetic faculty; that is, it brings things together (synthesizes) rather than breaks them apart (analyzes). In the second place, it is an image-making faculty; that is, its tendency is from the abstract toward the concrete, and not vice versa.

First, then, it synthesizes. It supposes, if only for the moment, a correspondence between wildly varying regions of experience. That is, it spies the quality in one object or situation which is also at work in the other, and by juxtaposing the two, it discovers something that is best seen (and perhaps *only* seen) by making the juxtaposition.

Here is a case in point of what I mean. We sometimes let our fancy stray into an elaborate associative activity. This happened to a man who was drooping on a bench in New York City's Washington Square one sultry July afternoon. Suddenly his wilting gaze was regaled by the approaching apparition of a borzoi.

What is this noble creature doing in this stifling purlieu? And on a chain to boot? Of all the dogs being walked in the park, this is the most anomalous. Here, through the dust and clutter, comes this royalty, this fleetness, this lean and coiled power. The long nose, the deep chest, the tail curled between the legs, the shaggy coat (not so heavy as his pajamaed Afghan cousin), the floating gait, the thin silhouette—he passes on his way like the Grand Duke in his progress. He does not waggle brightly at every passerby like lesser, more hopeful dogs. He is not asking for pats, scratches, and attestation from these people. He is not a good doggy; he is not a doggy at all. Every step is a potential spring, taken with that awesome grace that belongs only to restrained power, the same that you sense when a coloratura pauses on a mere F, or when Nureyev walks to the rear of the stage before a solo. He does not dart and sniff at every diversion. If he turns his attention to anything at all, it is a matter of deigning to do so, bestowing a ducal benison. He seems to have appeared only now from a feudal court, or from leaping across the steppes.

What is this evocative activity that is aroused by this dog? There is no court anywhere about. On the contrary, he has probably just emerged from a cramped row house in Washington Mews, or from the fifth-floor walk-up of some elegant clerk who wants an extravagant bibelot to take with him on his cruises in the park. Why does one imagine this creature surging across the steppes? He has probably never seen an open space wider than this square.

Some of the association, at least, is obvious. The dog is Russian, and we are likely to think of pre-Bolshevik—that is, tsarist—days in connection with something like this. Somehow, we do not imagine borzois on the hearth rug at the deliberations of the Presidium. There need to be velvet and damask and heraldry about. But this begs the question. Why, in our fancies, would we choose Peter the Great and not Khrushchev as the appropriate owner? The dog simply does not appear as a socialistic, or even a democratic, animal. His politics are distinctly hierarchic.

It is, of course, convincing enough to maintain that the locale of the evocative activity is in *me* and has nothing to do with the dog. Insofar as I choose to call up feudal Russian courts and boar hunts, I am at liberty to do so, but it has nothing to do with the dog. There is nothing implicit in the borzoi that demands such a setting.

And it would have to be admitted that this is so. You cannot establish a continuum between a given arrangement of hair, skin, and cartilage and a certain place and time in history. Or, pushing it further back, it is not possible to read feudalism in a special combination of calcium, carbon, hydrogen, and whatever else the dog is made of (I do not know my organic chemistry). Which is to say that the analytic knowledge of a given phenomenon yields little to our associative—that is, imaginative—perception. The man who would argue that you are being elfin by pursuing this line of thought would have at the same time to admit that *poetically* there is nothing grotesque about associating the borzoi and the Grand Duke, whereas there *is* something jolting about locating the borzoi scavenging among the garbage pails in an alley. (To be sure, this might be a redundant picture, but the jolt involved would be consciously sought by the poet, the idea being, What an unhappy juxtaposition, or How the mighty have fallen, or Look at the ironies of urban life.)

Again, it is simple enough to point out that the association of borzois and grand dukes is a matter of memory: we have read of them in connection with Russian history or seen them in a tapestry or a movie, and hence the association. If we had seen pugs or chihuahuas we would have made that association and not this.

But having admitted that, we may turn to another level and ask what it is about the presence of this dog that evokes certain ideas and not others. Unless we are being difficult, we would have to admit to a sense of *awe*. Whereas a beagle puppy sets us to boobling baby talk ("Aaah—he wad a tweet little puppy dog!"), and a Doberman frightens us, and a basset looks doleful, the borzoi takes our breath away. For one thing, there is the matter of proportion: he is *big* among dogs (and for this reason, a Saint Bernard or an Irish wolfhound also takes our breath away). But he is not especially big among animals. If we saw a horse that small, we would coo and cuddle the precious pony. Similarly, if we saw a mouse the size of a chihuahua, we would flee screaming. Because we have a general notion of dogness and of the size appropriate to that category, the borzoi appears as big to us.

Then again, he is *fleet*. Those long legs and that thin silhouette imply the ability to run. The fact that we

know he is a hunting dog confirms our suspicion that
he must be able to run. And he is *strong*. There is
nothing of the bulging muscularity of the English
bulldog here, or the sheer mass of the Pyrenees. But
those thin legs are not spindleshanks, and the weight-
less rhythm of the whole body as he walks suggests
power far in excess of what is being drawn upon at the
moment. We wonder if, besides all this, he is not *savage*. He may be as gentle as a lamb in his demeanor,
but when he yawns, we become aware that the potential of those grinning jaws and teeth is quite other than
the potential of the lamb's timid smile. We know that
we could plague a lamb into a frenzy, and the worst he
would do would be to try to wriggle away from us,
whereas we are not prepared to heckle a borzoi. Finally, he appears as *beautiful* to us. This is the most
elusive of all his qualities, and can be debated until we
are all black in the face. But the combination of shape
and color and size and bearing registers itself upon our
consciousness as beauty, for reasons that are as difficult to pin down as those which make the combination of shape and color and size and bearing in a hyena
register upon us as ugliness. We may begin, "Oh,
well, but the hyena skulks and the borzoi leaps", but
the question here is, for one thing, How do you *know*
the hyena is skulking? and, for another, In what sense
can it be insisted that leaping is higher on the scale of
muscular movement than skulking? Perhaps what appears to us as skulking is seen by hyena eyes as a regal
progress anyway. In any case, whatever hyena sensibility may be, the borzoi appears, presumably, as beautiful to *us*.

He appears to us, then, as big, fleet, strong, savage, and beautiful. The suggestion of magnitude, speed, strength, savagery, and beauty involuntarily arouses in us corresponding images of royalty. If he is not a king among dogs (perhaps the Saint Bernard or the German shepherd is this), he is at least a duke. Why? Because magnitude, speed, strength, savagery, and beauty are qualities that seem both appropriate to, and implicit in, the idea of royalty. To be sure, a prince may be small (Alexander the Great), but then he must somehow communicate royalness in spite of this, not because of it. His minitude is an exception to the whole image, and may be canceled by an imperial mien that sets all the hulking courtiers to shaking. We feel that the great size of a Richard Coeur de Lion, or a Frederick Barbarossa, is most fitting to the office of prince. Likewise with speed. Not that we ask our kings to be great track stars. But there is something ineluctable about the picture of the snorting stallion or the whirling chariot as more fit for the king than the dray horse or the oxcart. The idea of strength, of course, is so involved in the notion of royalty as to be nearly synonymous. And savagery. Again, not that we want tantrums and brutishness in our monarchs. But it is felt that there is terror behind the beneficent royal brow. Implicit in the idea of royal authority (this is strange to us who know only the wheylike authority of the committee) is an augustness which is not to be chucked under the chin. And beauty. If, besides the beauty that surrounds the royal presence in any case, the prince has a beautiful face, we are glad, for then we can see before our very eyes the correspondence

between royal office and royal person that we so ear-
nestly want to see, rather than having to keep insisting, as would be the case with an ugly prince, that it
is an inner beauty that counts (which it is, of course,
but we are speaking here of the appropriateness of *appearances* and of their influence on our sense of things).

So the borzoi passes on his way, and we, for whatever reasons, think of him as somehow prominent
among dogs, and it is not far from the idea of promi-
nence to the idea of preeminence, and from there to
royalty. For, even though we are creatures of a democratic frame of mind in this century, this dog does not
conjure for us images of the committee member.

This associative activity is, in a way, the opposite of
that which is at work in the scientific method. In that
method, the procedure is to take whatever is under
scrutiny (strata of rock, sexual aberration, blood),
and, by dismantling it, to get at the truth of the matter. It is the procedure, again, that has made possible
the modern commonplace "Well, of course we know
that it's *only* . . . ", the implication being, for instance, that, since what keeps the earth in place in the
stellar system is thus and so, it follows that Atlas *isn't*
holding it up; that is, that something *more true* about
the nature of things is being said when we talk of
gravity and centrifugal force than when we talk about
Atlas.

The imagination, on the other hand, handles things
not by boring into them but by casting about for correspondences from other regions of experience. So
that, confronted with, say, the furrowed brow of an
angry man, the analytic faculty would scrutinize the
muscular activity and the emotional turbulence and

ponder the cause–effect situation, whereas the imagination (the synthetic faculty) might see in miniature here something that seems also to be at work in meteorology and might come up with some such observation as "a visage like a thundercloud".

What is gained by yoking these two things? By evoking the thundercloud, the imagination has not, to be sure, said anything about the frown that can be extracted *from the frown itself*, but it has heightened our appreciation of the significance of the frown. And where is the special fitness of this frown-thundercloud juxtaposition? We would not feel that a frown-fog or a frown-mist equation would do, even though fog and mist are forms of water vapor as much as a thundercloud is. But they won't serve because the correspondence which is being observed here by the imagination has nothing to do with dampness or diffuseness or whatever else is suggested by water vapor. The appropriateness of the metaphor cannot be uncovered by probing either frowns *or* thunderclouds analytically. It exists in the realm where frowns and thunderclouds appear as exhibitions of the same thing, and it is not a realm which can ever be discovered with charts and telescopes and syllogisms.

But how, then, *do* the frown and thundercloud appear as exhibitions of the same thing? It must be something like this: a thundercloud announces a turbulent and frightening event to us, an event accompanied by noise and flashes and torrents of water, all of which taken together threaten destruction. Similarly, a frown is the token of wrath, which raises the possibility of broken furniture or perhaps the rod, or at least disapproval, all of which are forms of destruction. Fog and mist do not suggest this sort of thing. They have their own entail of suggestiveness—they shroud (shroud?) things, and muffle them, and bring obscurity and isolation and clamminess. This is a different array of suggestions from that entailed by the thundercloud.

As the imagination is a synthetic faculty in the first place, it is, secondly, an image-making faculty; that is, its tendency is from the abstract toward the concrete. It takes vague or difficult or elusive things and seeks a concrete embodiment of what it wants to say about them. This is, of course, almost inseparable from what we have just been talking about, that is, the synthetic faculty. For the synthetic process *is* the process that reaches out for the concrete example, or, put the other way, the image-making faculty finds the appropriate image precisely *by* looking around for correspondences in other regions of experience. To speak of the imagination, then, as an image-making faculty as opposed to a synthetic faculty is simply to focus differently on it.

We may take the example of the dishrag again. The thing in question, really, is my feeling of exhaustion. But this is an abstraction, and an abstraction has no force in it. I want, however, to get across to you how *very* tired I feel. I want you to have an intense awareness of my feelings. I want you to share as fully as possible in the experience. And so I look for the thing in some other region of experience that will suggest in itself, without adding any adjectives, what I feel. A dishrag is the very thing. There is nothing crisp about a dishrag. We do not need to specify that it is limp and damp and wrung out. That is in the nature of the rag—to be limp and damp and wrung out. The rag, in other words, embodies entirely satisfactorily the particular thing that I want to say at the moment. I do not need to go beyond the rag and itemize what it is that I am suggesting. Nor do I need to distinguish which properties of the rag I am calling upon (limpness rather than squareness, say). The image explains itself.

Image making is what delights us about certain people's conversation. I had a friend in England who used to amuse me again and again with this sort of thing. Once, when I went with him to his church, a man sitting near us sang the chants in a loud and peculiar buzzing voice. My friend leaned over, finally, and whispered in chagrin, "He sounds like a bee in a jam jar!" On another occasion, when he and I were out on the playing fields coaching some boys in preparation for the end-of-term sports day, a certain boy was practicing the standing broad jump near us. "Why, he jumps like a frog in a marsh!" gasped my friend.

It is not only in the amusing asides of conversation that imagination works. The habit we have of resorting to it all the time may suggest something about the nature of things and language that is far more radical than we might at first suspect. For the effort to clarify and intensify by finding an image is at work on all levels of communication. We shall talk more presently about poetry, which is the most finely wrought instance of the effort. But it appears everywhere. In business correspondence, a man may speak of a boom-and-bust cycle. In military affairs there are two-pronged thrusts and softening-up operations. In mathematics there are trapezoids and so many bags of

peppermints and *x*. In sociology there are peer groups
and upward mobility. In politics there are ghettos and
running for office. In society there are coming out and
climbing ladders. In theology God is at least *in here* if
he is not up there or out there (and the entire Christian scheme of creation and Incarnation is a case in
point that someone—God, in this case—is clarifying
and intensifying our apprehension of something by
getting an image that manifests whatever it is that is to
be manifest). The habit suggests that our whole apprehension of things occurs under the species of concrete
analogy, and that no thought or utterance at all is possible in any other terms. Even in symbolic logic, exactness and distinction are sought by supposing that
we may evoke *this* (some quantity or idea) in terms of
this (some squiggle on the paper).

Before looking at poetic language, however, we may
note the way in which imagination works in organizing our experiences, both unnoticeable daily functions
and the great pinnacle experiences of life.

Chapter Three

Lunch and Death

"Lunch won't be a ceremonial meal today." My wife said this to me one day recently when, because of various activities afoot, we had a quick sandwich in the kitchen and did not bother to sit down at the table.

A small aside in the course of the day, but one which touches upon something that is so present with us that, like eyesight and hearing, we almost never pause to look at it, or to think what life would be like without it. It is this: on all levels, from the lunch table to the coronation, we dispose our experience ritually. The panoply with which we surround all the common functions of daily life eludes analysis. That is, if we scrutinize the way we do things, we shall find that we have festooned everything with formality and that nearly every act is loaded down with gestures that bespeak much more than can be discerned in the functional demands of the situation itself.

For instance, we shake hands. Nothing is gained by this, at least nothing utilitarian. It is pure ceremony. Here come two primates pell-mell on the business of the day. As they approach one another, each extends an extremity and they interlace briefly. Neither of them needed an assist over a mud puddle or help with a heavy package. Nothing appears to have been gained by this. If we were to ask them what they were about, they would say, "We were shaking hands." Shaking hands? *Shaking hands*? What has that got to do with anything? What about wiggling toes? We don't understand what you brought about by the act. Do you do it every time? Or can you decide on the spur of the moment what dance you will do? No, no, we are told; it's just what people *do*. It doesn't accomplish anything. It's just what we do.

Just what we do. Exactly. "Just what we do" is to acknowledge, by tokens that are difficult to derive from the bare necessities of the moment, something that is at work in the moment, and that lies underneath whatever else is going on. In the case of a handshake, there is no clear functional connection between what our hands do and what we *mean* by it (which is "Hello, I see you, I grant your existence, I honor you", and so on). Presumably an anthropologist or historian might tell us the cultural origins of the handshake, and in those origins there might be observable some function. But whatever the function was, it has long since ceased to operate *as* that function, and exists as a ritual residue. For instance, if it could be shown that Cro-Magnon men grasped each other's forearms to fend off the possibility of a sudden blow from the other, then we would know the functional origin of handshakes. But the passage of centuries somehow mollified these pugnacious potentialities, and the act, while no longer necessary for the preservation of life and limb, remained. This, of course, may not be the case, but handshakes started somewhere, and, whatever they were once upon a time, they aren't necessary now. But they signal something, so we carry on with the ritual. It is as good a way as any of saying a great deal without wasting time going through verbal protestations of honor. And so there *is* a function to the ritual: it "means" that we recognize and greet the other person.

Or again, we set the table for a meal. Now presumably the function involved in eating is nourishment, and this asks only the transfer of food from point A (the garden or the shelf or the stove) to point B (our stomach). But we raise this function to fantastically elaborate heights by ritualizing it.

It is easy enough, in the case of a state banquet, to observe the panoply. The gold service (aluminum gets the food to your mouth as well), the crystal (pottery is sturdier), the flowers (you can't see the lady across the table), the lace (oilcloth is easier to clean), the candles (why must we squint when there are hundreds of watts in the ceiling?), and the rest. What is it all about? To say nothing of the *seating*. What, pray, is gained by worrying about whether the Minister Plenipotentiary of Borioboolagha ought to sit to the left or the right of the Honorable Mrs. Thigpen? There will be food, surely, at both places. Or why must the President and his wife sit *there*, and not over *here*? I'll wager they'd rather spend the evening with this wag over here than with the Earl of East Cupcake. What is this rigid, invisible, and benign tyranny to which the company subjects itself?

From the outside, of course, it is great fun to comment on the externalities of any ritual at all. To a democrat, the maces, ermine, and trumpets of monarchy look funny. To a Low Churchman, the murmuring, shuffling, and gesticulating of High Churchmanship look precious. To a Baptist, the Low Churchman's cassock, kneeling pads, and rote prayers look suffocating. To a secularist, the Baptist's Sunday clothes, testimonies, and choir look tragicomic. To Madison Avenue, Bleecker Street looks like a charade; to

Bleecker Street, Madison Avenue looks like a charade. To the penthouse cocktail party, the Sunday school picnic looks dull; to the Sunday school picnic, the cocktail party looks dull. It is always possible from the outside of a given situation to see the ritual as funny. If you do not grant the things which are understood as significant inside the circle, of course the ways in which that significance is acknowledged will appear as funny to you. If you don't understand, for instance, any idea of precedence in human affairs, then of course you will want to sack the chief of protocol and let people scramble for chairs. You may, of course, grant a precedence of *merit* (as opposed to heredity) so that you would seat the man who has *done* something at the head table rather than the old earl, but this is only an operational matter. You don't disagree with the aristocrat over the idea of precedence but only over the *warrant* for precedence (personal achievement versus birth). Nor do you disagree with him that precedence may legitimately be signaled by something that has nothing in the world to do with it, namely, by putting him here and not there at some table. He can get as much good food in the kitchen. Or, if you think Moslems are being silly to knock their foreheads on the rug, you must admit that your view does not exclude a man's doing other odd things with his body (standing aside for a lady, shaking hands, pounding the table) by way of acknowledging significance. You must admit that it is only the particular posture of the Moslem that strikes you as being silly, and that you have not bothered to ask what might make a busy modern man do it.

Any criticism of ritual arrives not from a nonritualist (there are none) but only from another sort of ritual. That is, I may say that such and such a ritual looks childish to me (I find it hard, for example, to see the costumes and liturgies of secret societies as serious). But two things need to be said here. In the first place, it is not the idea of ritual itself that I am criticizing, in that I myself can't walk ten steps without doing something ritually (again, standing aside for a lady, waving to a friend, lowering my voice in a museum). And in the second place, I would have to admit that the ritual that I see as silly probably proceeds very logically from the special set of ideas held by the people in that circle (in the secret society, say), so that their bibs and tassels and most reverend titles make perfect sense *given their set of categories*. If, then, I want to expose them as silly, I will have to show not that their ritual is silly but that their prior ideas are silly. If, for instance, there really *is* no basis for supposing that a given talisman has any mystic virtue attached to it, then the man who hallows it is either misled or pigheaded.

Having said this, however, one other thing may remain to be said: it might be possible to show that, even granting the prior set of categories from which some ritual springs, that ritual has nevertheless sunk into bathos. For instance, even though I subscribe to the Christian vision of the world and therefore see concepts such as Incarnation and sacrifice and hierarchy as substantial ideas, there are forms of Christian ritual that look to me as though they had lost control. This may take the form of celebrating something that didn't seem to want celebrating (mere emotion, say), or of elevating some idea or thing to a place all out of proportion to its place in the whole scheme (the tears of the Magdalen, perhaps).

But back to eating. Take a simple meal, where things are not so dazzling as they are at the state banquet. Except in the most harried situations, there is more occurring than the mere swallowing of food. We mark this thrice-daily event with certain formalities, no matter how small. We put place mats down, or a cloth. We put the fork on the left, even though the chances are that we will pick it up with our right hand. We put the napkin by the fork and not by the knife, even though this serves very little clear functional purpose. If we have a drink, we may raise our glasses briefly. We wait until the others have been served before we tuck in. We prefer the food to be arranged neatly on the plate, and not jumbled together in a stew (unless of course it is a stew). We like a bit of color—carrots or tomatoes—in with the green. We like a *slice* of beef rather than a heap of scraps. We would just as soon that the bread not be torn and battered. We put the gravy into a boat and the jam into a pot, even though this means dirtying more dishes. The chances are that even when we are alone, we do not stand at the stove and fork our food out of the saucepan directly into our mouth.

The objection to this line of thought will come, of course, from someone who will say, "Oh, but I *do* do it that way. I do leave milk cartons about, and I love stand-up meals. We waste years of our lives going through all this mumbo jumbo when we could be just as happy and twice as productive doing things more simply."

The only answer to this objection is: very well, you may *be* the busy career girl or board chairman who has a glass of Metrecal or a pastrami sandwich at your desk. But whatever else it is that overrides, in your mind, the usual pattern of pause and formality with which we mark this business of eating, I'll bet you don't see this as the ideal meal. Even though you may be the brisk type who thrives on the sixteen-hour workday, I doubt if you will argue that we must rid ourselves of the panoply that complicates the transfer of food from the stove to our stomachs. If you do, of course, and await the day when mealtime will mean a quick stop by the coin machine for an intravenous shot of some elixir from a syringe, then your paradise is my hell and you will have to write your own book.

The point in this is, as I have said, that we dispose our experience ritually. That is, we subject the common functions of life to an ordering that does not always serve the idea of mere efficiency. We handle our experience in a way that both *imposes upon* and *draws from* it significance. It is, in a word, a matter of form and content—of taking the plain stuff of experience (content) and organizing it ritually (forming it). The activity arises from the same inclination in us that we saw at work in the image-making faculty—the inclination, that is, to get some sort of detachment from experience so that we can grasp it and articulate it, and not just undergo it. And not only this. It is the signal of our awareness that things are *worth* something—that they are significant. We dignify the merely utilitarian. We seek a heightened consciousness of experience via form. We move through our experience like figures in a solemn dance, for we are such creatures as hanker for significance, and we suspect that significance emerges only and always from the union of form and content.

This inclination (it is called imagination) works, then, on the ordinary level (lunch) and on the extraordinary (state banquets). It might be worthwhile to look at how it works in response to the most extraordinary of all human experiences, death. For here there is dramatized for us with peculiar force the sundering of what aesthetics calls form and content, and what we usually call body and spirit.

It is ironic that death can be called extraordinary, in that it is the most remorselessly ordinary event of all. It is, quite simply, inevitable. It happens to everybody. It has been going on now since the beginning of history. We can't pretend that it is unprecedented or unimaginable or unusual or any of the other things that go into the extraordinary. How, then, can we call it extraordinary?

It is extraordinary in that, although it has been occurring with tedious and implacable regularity since the beginning of human time, it is never ordinary for the only person who experiences it, the victim. For him, the first go-around is the last. He had witnessed it all his life, of course. He had read general statistics (so many war deaths, traffic deaths, heart-ailment deaths, suicides per year), and they were minimally stirring. He knew people who died—neighbors and colleagues—and this stirred him a bit. He knew other people who died—friends—very well, and this made him pause and perhaps grieve. There were other people—parents, a brother, or a child—whose deaths turned life into a horror. And, if he was supremely unlucky, he experienced the death of his most beloved, an event that has been called worse than death by us who can't quite know what we are saying.

But no matter what his experience of death had been up to his own venture into it, that venture was extraordinary. For, unlike other cold plunges, there was no way at all of getting his toe into the water and testing it out ahead of time. It was everything all at once, even if he had been deathly sick for months. That final cough and rattle, the wrench and then the stillness—these were unexampled. To say nothing of what lay on the far side of the tubes and needles and oxygen tents and pillows. The sturdy insistence by some brave voices that there is nothing on that side is at best fatuous; there is absolutely no way of knowing *that*. What the consciousness of that person is of his own death is a sheer blank to us all, religious or non-religious.

But this is not a case for immortality. It is about form and content, and ritual, and death. It is about how we respond to the phenomenon of death when it appears in the course of our experience.

The impact which that appearance has upon us (and from here on we are speaking of the death of someone else; there is no use talking of our own) is in direct proportion to the distance between ourselves and the victim, that is, in proportion to the force of our love for that person. But here again, the topic at hand is not even the private emotions we feel upon encountering death. It is the way in which we *give shape to the event ceremonially*.

At one end of the ceremonial spectrum there would be the cases of death where, for various reasons, no ceremony attends the event. In 1968 there was a terrible earthquake in Iran. Bodies had to be shoveled into trenches. Presumably every day of the world there are fires in the furnaces of morgues about which no one says much. And the cadavers in medical schools may well have missed any ceremonial exequies.

But where the human imagination is free to respond to the phenomenon of death—that is, where there is time and love—it does so ceremonially. The ceremony may range from the merest tightening of the jaw muscles at the news, to sixty seconds of silence, to a cocktail party with the urn on the mantel, to wailing and garment rending, to suttee, to a requiem mass. That part doesn't matter. The part that interests us here is that it is in the nature of the human thing to mark the experience formally, that is, to give some structure to this worst of events both in order to cope with it all and to dramatize ceremonially what we feel about it.

The particular shape of the ceremonies derives from the idea which the people involved have as to what has occurred. In cultures where it is felt that demons have taken the person away, there may be wild lamentation and efforts to placate the spirits. In Christendom, there is both the acknowledgment of human grief and the celebration of the triumph over death. In nonreligious circles there may be a stoic acceptance of the irrevocable and final. And, of course, there may be the hysterical effort to deny the reality of the event by various forms of illusion and euphemism.

But whatever the particular idea in the ceremony is, we mark this event most solemnly. We take an occurrence (someone's demise) and move through it ceremonially, just as we take another occurrence (the transfer of food from shelf to stomach) and move through *it* ceremonially.

And, whatever else we experience of death, we must confess that there is a sense in which we all apprehend it as grotesque. For here we have come across the most arresting of all instances in human experience of the divorce of form and content.

Up to this point we had known the person as a whole. He was a human individual who looked such and such a way, acted such and such a way, and thought such and such a way. We could carry on exchange with him, responding to him and expecting responses to us. But now there he lies. Or not he, but his body. *His* body? Then where is *he*? A body is not a human being; it is a corpse. Nor is a spirit a human being; it is a ghost. Nor is a human being the pasting together of a corpse and a ghost. A human being is an indivisible phenomenon which we encounter *as* body, but whose body we speak of as being animated and energized and filled with something that cannot be described in strictly bodily terms. But neither can it be "subtracted" from the body, for immediately we get a corpse and not a human being. By the same token, the various efforts to get at the thing inside the body (whatever it is, we can think of it *only* in bodily terms—"inside" and "thin" or "vaporous" or "transparent"—all qualities that describe solid matter, but we must resort to them when we want to suggest our idea of whatever it is about us that is *not* body)—the various efforts to get at the thing inside find themselves addressing ghosts and spirits and not human beings. The person you call up at the séance, if it is not the humbug sitting across the table from you, is hardly your lover; it is at best his ghost, his residue, his disfranchised semiself. Indeed, the very words we use when we encounter the sundering of the "parts" of a human being show our awareness of this sundering as not a mere mathematical subtraction, but as something grotesque, even terrible. When a human being is himself—that is, whole, or alive—we may speak of his body as his "figure" or "physique" and use such terms as "lithe" or "wiry". When he ceases, in the event called death, to be himself, we speak of that body as a corpse, and there are no good connotations in the word "corpse". It may be a lithe corpse, but then we experience that litheness only in terms of grotesque irony ("How awful that such a beautiful creature should *die!*"). The corpse presents us with an impalpable mystery: Is it, or is it not, our friend? We cannot settle for the simple dictum that it is not, for everything that we ever saw of him is there in the coffin and cannot be waved aside as nothing. All our affections and imaginings shout at us that it *is* he. But they shout just as loudly that it is not he at all. This silence, this impotence, this muffled defeat—it is not, it is not he. A plague take the monster who brought about this ambiguity. There would be no ambiguity if it were not for the simultaneous and powerful awareness of *him* and *not him*. This shape is, in effect, he; but the shape is *not* itself because, ironically, it is *only* itself. That is, in order for it to be authentically itself (i.e., a body and not a corpse), it had to be animated and brimming and quickened with something that was more than itself. The minute it became only itself— only the legs and arms and face—it ceased to be itself—that is, the form of a beautiful creature—and became the pillaged and vacated parody of that form. The desolation that loiters about a ruined castle is as nothing to this desolation, for the castle was merely peopled by beings who came and went up and down its corridors and staircases and sang in its halls and gave, as it were, life to its stone towers. When the noise ceased and silence settled in, the castle began to seem desolate. But it was a desolation that followed upon the subtraction of a perfectly clear "content" (crowds of royal children and retainers and stewards and pages) from a perfectly clear "form" (a stone edifice). The desolation is of course more intense in proportion to the liveliness of the content; that is, a ruined granary may have an air of loneliness about it, but not so intense an air of loneliness as a ruined banquet hall has, since the one edifice held at best bags of malt, while the other held great celebrations. But in the evacuation of a human being, you get not merely the leftover form haunted by memories of a fled content. You get grotesquery and dissolution. For, unlike the castle, the body existed *only* insofar as it was "populated". And even this is too remote a way of speaking of it, for it is not as though it had been populated with some visiting spirit; it *is* that spirit existing under the modality of time and space. It is the form of that spirit, and not just the cage (or castle) of that spirit. And that thing, that whole thing, which we scrutinize under the dual modality of space-time (body, i.e., form) and identity (spirit, i.e., content), we call a human being. It is not ghost-plus-corpse. It is a whole from whose "form" you cannot subtract some "content" and still have anything. Only terror and grotesquery are left over.

And so, when we encounter this jolting event in the course of our affairs, we do not wave it off. We take it and shape it in the only way left to us—ceremonially. We cannot leave the event or our experience of it without any form. The grief, the awe, the fear, the silence, the perplexity, the ruin—we cannot leave these flying about in a windy clutter. We must take the whole thing and proceed through it formally. It takes time and money, but there is no question of dumping the refuse out like the coffee grounds and orange peels from breakfast. For even though we do not suppose that anything actual is gained for the victim by the slow cars and hush, yet we affirm the appropriateness of it all as the formal enactment of the human experience of death.

Shaking hands, setting the table for lunch or a banquet, funeral obsequies—these are cases in point of the imagination, the image-making faculty, at work. They are the carving in action, we might say, of human experience, just as sculpture is the carving in stone, or poetry the carving in words, of human experience; the articulation in *this* mode (stone or words or ritual) of something that appears in *this* realm (human experience); the whole effort energized by the invincible suspicion that the appropriateness we sense in establishing these correspondences is more than merely haphazard—indeed, that it might have something to do with the way things are: that everything means everything.

Chapter Four

"One Foot Up,
One Foot Down"

We have been talking about how we organize experience ceremonially. Poetry is an attempt to do this in language. It is an attempt in which the question of form and content becomes difficult, in that, on the one hand, it cannot be denied that there is a sense in which the poet *does* take raw matter (an event, an idea, an observation, an emotion) and shape that content by means of painstaking articulation; but then immediately you have a new *thing*—a poem—in which form and content are inseparable, indeed, indistinguishable, in that the poem is not a mere speaking *about* this (the content) in that special way (form). Rather, it is the formed matter, or the matter formed, and hence it is a new and distinct thing, with its own identity. Just as lunchtime, although it involves the matter of getting food from point A to point B, is a qualitatively different thing from the intravenous injection of nourishment. That is, in both cases (poetry and ceremony) a new thing has appeared from the union of form and content, a thing which arrays the materials in such a way as to yield a sense of significance—a significance not foreign to those materials, but rather inherent in them. Hence, it may be worthwhile looking at the way in which poetic language does, in its way, what ceremony does.

For it is in poetry that human speech makes the supreme effort to approximate what our imagination leads us to suspect is, in fact, the way things are. Put another way, it is in poetry that we try to speak the language that is suggested to us by our imagination as the real language of things. Or, put still another way, we do in poetry exactly what we do when we set the table for lunch or see a borzoi as an image of royalty: we acknowledge that the abstraction wants *shape*—that the dog *may* without foolishness be apprehended as an instance of what also appears in princes; that the ritual enacting of the business of nourishment alone exhibits the true significance of what is occurring; that the measure, cadence, exactness, and economy of poesy raise language to its highest power.

In other words, poetic language tends *toward* the way things are, and not away from it; or at least the old myth would have had it thus.

This is a view which is exactly the opposite of the popular view of poetry. Poetry, it is believed, is a fanciful diversion, a charming way to escape briefly from the real business of life. Politics and commerce and urban planning and medicine and housekeeping—here is where the real stuff is. Insofar as we stumble across a bit of verse once a year or so—say, an ode to local heroes at the town cenotaph on the Fourth, or a limerick—this is fine. But there is nothing here to engage the attention of the busy modern man. What with the awful pressures of professional life and breadwinning and family plus the frightening actualities of contemporary events—civil revolution, the Bomb, the dollar—there is little time left to read about nymphs and shepherds, or fops languishing over posies.

Who could quarrel with this? And yet there is an irony. For with all the frightening march of contemporary life, we still read of Little Miss Muffet and Wee Willie Winkie to our children, and sing "Here We Go Round the Mulberry Bush" and "Sing a Song of Sixpence". But this is all wrong. What are we doing? Are we trying to cozen them by leading them to believe that there are joy and naïveté and rhythm in life, when all the time we know that their whole experience of life will be a relentless dashing of all these notions? Aren't we deceiving them with these pictures of simplicity and quaintness, setting up the conditions for disenchantment? Why not be honest with them? Why not Sing a Song of the Devaluated Pound, or of Little Herr Hitler? Better yet, why sing a *song* of anything? Why not read a column from the *Times*? Wouldn't it be more realistic, to say nothing of more merciful, to begin early to brace them for what life is really all about, rather than beguiling them with all this trumpery, knowing full well that it is fraudulent?

Most of us, if pressed on this, would not have thought of any very cogent defense for nursery rhymes. They would not have occurred to us as something that needed any particular rationale. Why do we read them to our children? We just *do*, that's all. They are what is in the books that we buy in the children's section. And besides, they are *nice*, aren't they?

Upon a little further reflection, we might find ourselves arguing that, so far from the devaluated pound and Herr Hitler and the columnists being the real stuff of life, they are the ephemerae, the things which come and go with the decade, and that it is not these which we wish to plow into our children's early imagination as being of the essence. Not that we wish to cheat them with bright tales that were never true of any world; but we suspect that there is a view possible, and that it is a view not far from the truth of the matter, that would see the great wars and political campaigns and current agonies as squalls on the surface of human existence, and that, whether the issue of the moment is Attila the Hun or the South Sea Bubble, or Taxation without Representation, or apartheid, there are constants in human experience that lie underneath these. This is not to say that these squalls are trivial and may not swamp us. Here is one of the ambiguities of existence—that we may be drowned by huge and impersonal movements that have nothing to do with us, so that we find we have lost our lover or our son or our leg because of political collisions from which we would far rather have been excluded. How many of the peasants of Europe had any quarrel with Attila, or had any idea who he was? Their lives did not in the least concern him, but this did not prevent their lives from being blasted in his furious advance.

Whatever else is asked of us by calamity, we find that we experience it as interruption. But in order for there to be an interruption, there must be a prior expectation. You cannot interrupt pure randomness. We naturally expect our lives to be more or less thus and so. "If I live and keep my health", we say, and might add, "and if the stock market doesn't crash, and war holds off, and drunken drivers keep their distance, and falling bricks fall there and not here, and I don't trip on this rug—if none of this happens, I will do so and so." It is this highly perilous "so and so" that we like to think of as the constant—things like eating and drinking with our family and friends, and talking and walking and listening to music and making plans.

There, then, is the ambiguity—that we must often come to terms with interruption as the only reality left to us. But what of the nursery rhymes? We cannot give our children death and desolation at bedtime (albeit Jack did break his crown). There will be time enough for them to face all that.

We are doing one of two things when we sing to our children. We are either indulging in a cynical duplicity that is only creating the conditions for disenchantment, or we are passing on to them, as we had passed on to us, something that the human imagination has sanctioned as being in some way perennially valid.

It will be objected here that this is all far too serious. You are reading too much into it all. No one is pretending to be doing anything but amusing the children with the nursery rhymes. I mean, Little Boy Blue—for heaven's sake, don't ask me to be singing about metaphysics when all I am doing is singing an innocuous song. Don't insist on seeing a cosmic order in Goosey, Goosey, Gander.

Touché. An argument like this can get too convoluted. The point that is being made is that, for reasons that are not always immediately clear, rhythm and fancy appeal to us. The imagination of childhood responds to the jog-trot account of incidents of very little importance. We keep the tradition alive, seldom inquiring into the genius of the tradition. The argument of this book is that there is in nursery rhymes a case in point of what the human imagination suspects—that the formal disposing of common things may not be misleading.

It may also be objected that I have missed the whole point by failing to see that it is precisely the *childish* imagination to which the rhymes appeal, and that the process of becoming adult requires the gradual dis- avowal of that fanciful world. You are not asking us, are you, to drop our board meetings and research and professional journals, and go a-maying into some fool's paradise? It is surely not that sort of thing that makes the world turn?

It is true that we must stop playing eventually and start learning our sums. The business of life seems to have little to do with the fancy that our childhood al- lowed us.

But there is the question. What, precisely, *is* "the business of life"? We can get onto an endless carousel if we try to decide which is the serious stuff of life, work or play. It is possible to take either view: either we toil away our eight hours so that we can get down to the real stuff—pleasure and love and recreation—or we enjoy periodic intervals of escape from the real stuff, the work. This vague oscillation goes on just be- low the surface in our consciousness, and we are never quite sure what it is we are, in fact, supposed to be doing. When are we wasting time—at the desk or on the beach? What was a man made for, when the chips are down?

A little probing reveals the superficiality of either view. We know that the real stuff of life cannot be lo- cated either at our desk or on the beach. Whatever it is, it won't be parceled out that way. Experience doesn't hold off while we are at work and begin when the whistle blows. *The whole thing* is "the real stuff", and the irony is that, unless we take ourselves by the scruff of the neck and make ourselves reflect upon it, we allow it to tumble past us helter-skelter and never grasp *any* of it as real. Here, parenthetically, is one of the losses sustained in growing up: it is in the nature of childhood to live fully in the moment, savoring the warmth of the sand or the dancing of the dust in the sunbeam or the new taste of raspberries, without emasculating the sensation by worrying over what has just occurred or what is about to occur. Adulthood, on the other hand, entails the pitiless awareness of time, which drains away our pleasures (much more rapidly, it always seems, than our pains), and hurries crisis and doom at its heels, so that at our painstakingly hus-banded and long-anticipated two-week Tyrolean idyll we are, alas, mostly aware of just that—that it is *two weeks*, and that the edelweiss and dirndls and alps are ours only momentarily and therefore in effect unreal. On the other hand, we find ourselves treading numbly through the other eleven and a half months as though the only real thing in the year were the holiday. What-ever there is about life that is substantial, it eludes us, like the egg in *Through the Looking-Glass.*

But there is, *mirabile dictu*, something in us that will not settle for this state of affairs. There is, it would almost seem left over from our childhood, the invinci-ble desire to locate experience and grasp it and savor it in the same way that we used to need to get hold of some new toy and handle it and get our teeth into it. This is pointless, we suspect—this carousel that spins us *past* things and never lets us get the ring.

And the faculty in us that shouts at us above the wheezing of the calliope that something *is* there, and that it is as full of texture and flavor and knobbiness as we wish it were—this faculty is imagination. It is imagination that stands like a Don Quixote against the whirling blades of time. It is imagination that plants in us in the first place the idea that the turning may be robbing us of our only chance to live, unless we find out that at the center of every turning there is a still point, and that we move toward that point in whose stillness there are held all the turnings that seem so helter-skelter to us.

And the language of this awareness that is in us all is the language called poetry. It is the language whose first halting utterances are our efforts to describe our experience by getting images of it from other realms of experience ("this sea breeze is a tonic"; "you're a doll"). It is the language, skipping or solemn, that elevates our experience by imposing a form upon it, not arbitrarily, but because it suspects that the truest way of speaking of that experience is formally. It is the language that, in effect, sets the table for lunch, that is, that disposes and arrays the common stuff of experience so that it is ritually transfigured from mere function into an instance of glory.

For it is the language that takes a serious view of experience. It is not satisfied with the idea of mere random tumble. It is *not* mere random tumble, it insists. There is something here. There is something to be said. There is something, oddly, to be elicited from this tumble. Take it. Grasp it. Handle it. Try one thing and another. Try to shape it. Impose some form on it. Lo . . . lo . . . when you are finally satisfied that you have imposed the right form on it, you will wonder whether that form was imposed by you or whether it emerged from the thing itself.

This is the business of the poets. They are the burdened and happy spirits who can do this—this that we all try to do. Burdened because they know that the most important thing is the most daunting thing—to seek and find and utter that significance that emerges from the union of form and content; happy because from time to time they succeed.

What is the nature of this language—this language that supposes that the truest way to speak of experience is to speak formally? Why should we be asked to read about things that hardly seem to bear on modern life (Trojan wars and things) in language that is anything but colloquial? What claim does the hero Beowulf have on me? Why am I to take time away from television and the newspaper to read of William's *Vision Concerning Piers Plowman*? And especially in language that is nearly indecipherable? Sir Philip Sidney may well have been "fain in verse" his "love to show", but, to begin with, I have my own love troubles, and moreover, I don't want to read about his *in verse*. It's all very well for George Herbert to have gone on about Easter wings and things, but suppose I share neither his categories (resurrection and all that) nor his crotchety language? Now Wordsworth and Keats— that's a bit better, and I don't object to reading about a flower or a vase in a moment of idleness, but don't harry me with it and try to tell me that it's anything that should arrest me. And as for modern poets, they can't be decoded anyway.

What is it like, this poetic language?

If it is possible to sort out one element that would be common to all poetry from Homer to our contemporary poets, it might be the element of formality. That is, no matter what poetry talks *about*, it talks about it in a special way, and it is a matter of supreme importance to any serious poet, ancient or contemporary, to get that way just right. The language must be lifted away from the contingency of mere conversational chitchat (even though some poets—Wordsworth or Whitman, for instance—have tried hard to get the rhythms of ordinary speech; but that is just the point: they had to *try hard* to get the effect they wanted; they did not just transcribe conversation). There are a thousand devices that poets use to achieve what they want, and it would take a whole book, if not a whole shelf of books, just to talk about rhyme, rhythm, ellipsis, inversion, metaphor, economy, precision, and so on— all the things at the disposal of poets to help them say *what* they want *how* they want to say it.

To illustrate the nature of poetic language, and, more important, to see how it is a case in point of the imagination at work, we might look at a very uncomplicated bit of verse.

It is not as though you have said the same thing about a walking experience when you say, "One foot up, one foot down, / That's the way to London town", and, "It is possible to walk to London." There may be a point of contact, to be sure, in that both sequences of words touch on the matter of getting to the city. But it is no more significant a point of contact than is the similarity, say, between kneeling to pray and kneeling to tie your shoe. The similarity, that is to say, is not such that it throws any light on the nature of either thing. When you say, "One foot up, one foot down, / That's the way to London Town", you have done more than suggest a method of transportation. You have evinced *a kind of experience*. And you have evinced that kind of experience not by the number or the oddity or the brilliance of the words you have used in your statement. Every word there is a monosyllable (except for the name London itself), and not only that, but a monosyllable that would probably appear in a list of the one hundred most common words in the language. And it is a very brief statement. There is no talk of the scenery on either side of the road—quaint inns and stiles and hedgerows (or factories and ash heaps and filling stations). There is no introduction or scenario (Who is making this trip? Are there alternative routes? Is this a hortatory or a merely declarative statement?). There are no descriptive adjectives to create an atmosphere. What, then, is the force of this sequence of words? Or, if "force" is too exalted a word for this jingle, the charm? Or at least the sticking power (it stays in our memory forever).

The force (let us call it that) of the sequence rises from several things. None of the things mentioned here, taken by itself, can account for the peculiar nature of the sequence. Moreover, the mere addition of these things to one another won't account for it either. It is like talking about a painting by Leonardo. You may talk about line and color and mass and light and subject matter and so on, but the whole which you are struggling to grasp is infinitely greater than what we would get if you or I were to follow the recipe that our study of the painting had yielded. This jingle is no Leonardo, to be sure, but it is *like* the Leonardo in that it is a formal utterance of simple experience.

The force of the jingle, then. It is highly specific. That is, instead of using even the perfectly clear and ordinary verb "to walk", it peers closely at the activity suggested in that verb and gives us, rather, the exact thing that occurs when we walk: one foot up, one foot down. If there is any other way of walking, we haven't discovered it yet, and the narrowing of focus to the muscular act of lifting one extremity and setting it down, then the other, then the other, all the way along the road to London arouses in us an awareness of the experience of walking that may have been worn down by the commonness of the verb by which we ordinarily designate it. The verb has become an almost purely functional and efficient way of getting on with the process of thought, with as little delay over details as possible. Moreover, there is a sort of bracing simplicity here: we won't shilly-shally over possible modes of transportation. We will lift one foot up and put the other one down, precisely as all men from the beginning of time have done if they wanted to get from one place to the other. It is a sort of martial summons away from hesitancy and indecision to the peremptory simplicity of the task at hand. It is as though we said, "This is the thing to be done, so let's get on with it *thus*."

But it is not just peremptory. It is fraught with levity. The job, that is, is not burdensome; it is light. There is a brisk joy in this most literally pedestrian of all human activities. This task that is unavoidable and mechanical and functional is, rightly savored, the occasion of joy. It is far more than the mere means of getting from point A to point B. It is a thing in itself, one of the great gifts to humankind, as any paraplegic would tell us. And how shall we grasp this joyous "thingness" of the old function? How shall we hail our harried minds and turn them to what they might miss? Well, one way is in the rhythmic swing of the little jingle. The lifting of one foot and the putting down of the other then becomes, in its physical mode, an occasion of exactly the same quality of joy that is evinced in the *poetic* version of the statement "It is possible to walk to London." That is, the *function* is transfigured into an instance of glory (What is better than walking? What do we *do* on a beautiful evening on our holiday if we have our wits?). So that the intense awareness of the joy of striding is to the function of walking from A to B as "One foot up, one foot down, / That's the way to London town" is to "It is possible to walk to London." And the quality of the experience is manifest in the rhythmic nature of the language. It is not as though the rhythm were a bit of salt. If it can be spoken of at all as something "added to" the prose statement (and I do not grant this), it is at least a magic powder that brings about a miraculous change in the old substance. But whatever it is, the rhythm makes possible the awareness of, *and is itself an instance of,* the particular glory of walking, a glory that is missed entirely when walking is understood only in its functional role as the vexing interval lying between our being at points A and B.

It does this by disposing words in a pattern of rising and falling that seems, above all, natural. We do not feel that the words have been squashed into some Procrustean bed here, and that they strain to get back into their own order and shape. Quite to the contrary, we have a sense of utter naturalness and inevitability, as though this were the exact order for which these words were made. They seem to be most perfectly themselves when they appear arrayed in this order. The adverb "up", for example, that gets lost in a thousand useful phrases every day, dances here in its special glory, for it is set about with the conditions that, like footlights and sets, isolate it for its solo, while at the same time placing it perfectly in relation to the other elements. It appears here not only as the lowly arrow designating such and such a direction, but also as the climax to a rhythmic rise ("One foot *up*"), and as the antiphon to its cousin, the other adverb "down". And the antiphon is itself dual: it is rhythmic ("one foot *up*, one foot *down*"—the anticipation set up in our imagination by the up demands the resolution of the *down*), and it is spatial (we can't leave our foot in the air—the process of walking goes ahead by the antiphonal sequence of up-down, up-down, all the way to London). The same sort of thing could be pointed out for any of the words in that first line: each appears most excellent and most individual precisely to the extent that it is harmoniously arrayed in relation to its neighbors. This is one of the paradoxes of poetic language and one which, according to the argument of this book, may both hint at, and itself be an instance of, the way things are.

And not only the poem (or the jingle) itself. What about our response to it? Oddly, we experience this formal elevation of an otherwise functional statement ("It is possible to walk to London") as delight. It stays with us forever. There is something in the nature of the language that activates a pendulum in our imagination; the swing of the words evokes the swing of the walk, and we find some swing inside of us answering to it. Our voice swings *up* and *down* as we read the line (try reading it in a monotone: admit it—you have to force it). If we are reading it aloud to a child, we shall probably find ourselves cocking our head from side to side, the nods corresponding exactly to the rhythmic rising and falling of the line: "*One* (nod left) foot *up* (nod right), one (nod left) foot *down* (nod right again)". We may even abandon caution to the point of pounding our knee with our fist and tapping our foot. And there is no confusion about any of it. It does not come out: "One foot (tap) up, one (nod) foot (pound) down".

Why we should experience rhythm as delight is a nice question, and the attempt to answer it fully here would land us squarely in a quarrel involving everything from psychology to eschatology. But something can be said. It may have something to do with satisfaction. I should think there are at least four kinds of satisfaction aroused by rhythm: the satisfactions of resolution, of recurrence, of recognition, and of transfiguration (the alliteration is wholly coincidental; I am not trying for a further kind of satisfaction).

Resolution. There is an expectancy set up in any rhythmic interval, as though we were holding our breath (breathing is itself a case in point), and when that expectancy is not rewarded, trouble results. If, for instance, we become unable to follow the rhythmic pattern of inhaling and exhaling, death results. Every breath drawn in anticipates the momentary discharge of that breath, and every discharge anticipates an immediate refilling. Again, every dawn expects a twilight, and every dusk a daybreak. When men find themselves in polar nights with no dawn at all for weeks at a time, the restlessness and depression brought on by this interrupted rhythm must somehow be offset. Again, sleep is good only insofar as it follows and precedes waking: when we slip into torpors and comas, our friends are alarmed over the interrupted rhythm. Obversely, insomnia is a plague that makes our waking a horror. The rhythm in poetic language is this same anticipation-resolution antiphon appearing under the species of words. The anticipation in "One foot . . ." needs the resolution of "*up*". We can't be kept holding our breath forever, but the nature of the thing makes us hold it until something comes along, in this case the adverb. Further, the larger anticipation set up in the sequence "One foot up" needs the resolution of the answering "one foot down", and beyond that, the whole line "One foot up, one foot down" needs the next line, "That's the way to London town." Beyond that we need nothing. We do not wait for further help. The thing is complete, resolved. And we experience this completeness as satisfaction.

Recurrence. This is, perhaps, the other side of the resolution coin, in that it involves the periodic appearance of something, but the particular satisfaction here is not so much that of the relaxation made possible by the rewarding of anticipation as the fascination of repetition. It is a paradoxical fascination, in that it entails both the arousing and the lulling of attention. For example, all of us find our attention aroused at first by some instance of repetition: a pile driver hammering remorselessly at its work, the solemn ticktock of a great clock, surf bashing on the rocks, a drop of water plopping from the roof gutter into a puddle, the thrust of pistons in some huge engine. We watch it, rapt. The regular recurrence of the motion and the sound summons something in us, and we attend. Here is an engaging diversion from the random clutter round about. It is strangely compelling, and strangely satisfying. That piston thrusting in and out, in and out, hiss–clank, hiss–clank, keep–it–up, keep–it–up, bravo-bravo, don't-stop, don't-stop, always-always . . . before long we are mesmerized, and the thing that had aroused our attention is now lulling us with a spell.

The rhythm of poetic language is this same recurrence, appearing again under the species of words. Whatever it is about recurrence that fascinates and satisfies us, it hails us also from poetic language. "The As*sy*rian came *down* like a *wolf* on the *fold*, / And his *co*horts were *gleam*ing in *pur*ple and *gold*"—this is something vastly different from, and better than, "The Assyrian army, with all its flags and armor glittering, pounced on the Israelites as a wolf attacks a sheepfold." The latter is not bad at all, but it is not in a class with the former. The regular beat of the words in the former not only evokes the rapid and relentless approach of the invaders' horses; it is itself a case in point of recurrence, and the recurrence fascinates us. The Israelite boy stands thrilled and horrified by the approaching tempo; the reader of Byron's poem finds himself caught up in the same thrill and horror. Similarly, in the jingle about getting to London, the tump-tump-tump-tump, tump-tump-tump-tump of the two lines arouses us more than would the prose statement of the same fact. And, presumably, it would eventually lull us, as would the very anapaest of Byron's poem itself.

Recognition. Again, it is only an aspect of what is implied already in resolution and recurrence. There is something peculiarly satisfying about discovering (recognizing) that *this* is like *this*—that what we un-earth over there is a case in point of what we have found to be true over here. For instance, we find our-selves fascinated watching a fly preen and groom itself—or do whatever it is that we interpret as preening. "Why, *we* do that! It's almost human!" we exclaim, and the fly is to that extent more interesting to us than he might be if we could see nothing in him that reminded us of ourselves. Similarly, we watch a raccoon fastidiously washing his food and are de-lighted over this action that seems more "human" than animal. And in the case of dogs we cannot help but see in their facial expressions the same emotions (joy, wistfulness, disappointment, shame, hope, guilt) that we register with our own facial expressions. And the peculiar satisfaction of recognition not only oper-ates with respect to things that reflect ourselves to us; wherever we come across a case in point of something that we already know, or that reminds us of another realm, we experience this satisfaction. Sometimes in a foreign country we will come upon a vista that re-minds us of something at home. "Oh, look at this view over here; it's exactly like Franconia!" and there is a particular quality of pleasure that attaches to this, even though there may be other areas that are more spectacular or quainter. Likewise, in a film, if we sud-denly realize that we have been at the very spot where the action is taking place, we have to pass the word along to the others in the group: "Psst! I've been *right there!*" Certainly part of the pleasure of baroque music is that again and again we recognize this bit here as a repetition or reworking of that bit there. And how many times have we found ourselves fascinated with a face in a crowd that looks exactly like someone we know? Even after we discover that it is not our friend, we keep stealing glances at it, curiously drawn to this familiar and yet different thing.

This is part of the pleasure of rhythm in poetic language, I should think. For we recognize in the rising and falling of the verse itself something that answers directly to the matter at hand, a case in point of what is being bespoken by the poem, in fact. This is obvious enough in matters like the Assyrian descending on the Israelites (the rhythm is *like* the hoofbeats), or in the "one foot up, one foot down" (we can keep step with the verse as we walk along). That is, there is something brisk in human experience that appears in various situations and under various guises (horses' hoofs, marching tempo) that satisfies something in us, and we recognize the same thing at work here in this poem. And it does not strike us as having been forced upon the poem; rather, the poem is unimaginable without it. It seems to rise from the stuff of the poem quite inevitably.

But it not only obtains where there is a perfectly recognizable similarity between the beat in the lines of verse and footsteps or hoofbeats or whatever is being talked about. The same principle is at work as well in situations where there is no obvious beat involved. Take Wordsworth's lines: "It is a beauteous evening, calm and free; / The holy time is quiet as a nun", and so on. Presumably if the rest of us had been with him on that evening walk with the little girl, we would not have been particularly conscious of any *pulse* throbbing in the scene before us, save for the irregular wash of the surf on the shore. So there is no very obvious demand for a regular rhythm in a description of the impression here. But the poet has ordered his lines into a rigorous pattern of rising and falling. It is the most common pattern in traditional English poetry (it is called iambic pentameter), and it can be argued of course that this pattern was there, ready for Wordsworth's hand, and so he simply used it. He didn't draw it from his subject matter by some incantation. It was just a poetic convention, and he used it again and again, no matter what his subject was. Don't maintain, please, that iambic pentameter has anything more than an incidental relationship with this beauteous evening calm and free.

But I will maintain it. There is the paradox of poetry. What seems to have been imposed rather arbitrarily by the poet (couldn't he have used dactyls?) ends up seeming to rise from the stuff itself, and appears to be not only the best but the *only* form under which he could have said exactly what he said. Of course he could have used a thousand other forms, but then the thing would not be the same. It would not even be an alternative way of making some statement *about* a beauteous evening. For Wordsworth's sonnet is more than a formalized comment about an evening walk (just as a lunch at a perfectly set table is more than a fancy way of what could be done as well with an intravenous injection). It is a thing itself, and a thing which answers to a quality implicit in this beauteous evening, but which we would miss without the midwifery of the poet. In the restraint under which the words are held by the demands of the rhythm, there is a case in point of the restraint that under another mode seems to be imposed on the fever of human activity by evening. In the measured evenness of these iambs there is exhibited a sense of what we also think we apprehend about evening. Evening does not exist in our imagination as a higgledy-piggledy time. The figure of Evening in pageants is not likely to be a henwife or a scold; it is probably a tall, gray-robed lady, austere, benign, and quiet. Her pace is measured and even, and so is the language in which Wordsworth speaks of her (i.e., the nun in the second line of the sonnet).

So much, then, for recognition. It cannot be pressed too far, else we shall find ourselves hunting for iambs under every bush. It is not that. Rather, it is simply that, in the restraint and measure of the rhythm Wordsworth chose here, there seems to be a case in point of what he was addressing himself to. Or, put another way, whatever other ways there might be of speaking of evening (and there are a thousand), none could be truer or more appropriate than this. We become aware, by virtue of the rhythmic language, of something that the poet is pointing out about the evening. This is an antiphon: like is calling to like, from the sonnet to the evening, from Wordsworth's impression to us, and so on.

Finally, transfiguration. Take again the jingle about getting to London. Unless we are on a holiday outing, the business of getting to the city is pure business and plays not only a subordinate role in our idea of what is important about the day but probably a boring role as well, i.e., "Today we'll get up at 7:00 so we can be in the city by 10:00 and have an early start." *Getting* there is a minus quantity ordinarily; it is only time subtracted from what we might otherwise be doing if we

could flit from here to there instantly. If we do anything at all with the trip, we probably try to fill in the
interval by doing something *other* than traveling: going
to the dining car for coffee, or reading the morning
paper, or playing "I'm thinking of something red"
with the children. The trip itself is purely functional
and exists in our minds, therefore, if it exists at all, as
meaningless. It is one of the items crowding our daily
experience that does not seem to be part of the real
stuff. It is only a functional thing, and exists only between this and that—between, say, breakfast and the
city. But if we scrutinize our rushed assumptions im-
placably enough, it appears that everything we do is
"only" functional, and that we are entangled in a mass
of threads that are being drawn not into a pattern but
into a knot that will throttle us one fine day.

But then the poet turns his attention to this common and cluttered stuff of daily experience, and it all
suddenly becomes significant. Even on the "low" level
of nursery rhyme, this transfiguration of the functional into something worthy appears. Take the old
rhyme about the days of the week:

> I went to visit a friend one day,
> She only lived across the way,
> She said she couldn't come out to play,
> 'Cause Monday was her washing day.

Refrain: This is the way we *wash* our clothes, etc.,
etc.

Now the washing of clothes is hardly one of life's
ecstasies, no matter what the detergent ads on television tell us. It is something that has to be done every

week, and there is no romance about it. But then there is this peculiar celebration of washing clothes in the nursery rhyme. The job becomes the occasion of a certain delight. The little glimpse of life in that verse is a glimpse into a picture where the necessities of life dance in a pattern of harmonious activity. There is a rhythm to the whole picture (i.e., on Tuesday we iron, on Wednesday we bake, and so on, round to next Monday), and a rhythm to the thing itself: "*This* is the way we *wash* our clothes, *wash* our clothes, *wash* our clothes", *scrub*-scrub, *down*-and up, *down*-and up. It is the worst kind of washing—with a washboard instead of a Westinghouse. And it may be argued that this is a grossly false picture and that nothing of this sort ever worked on this earth. But that is not true. Grant that ninety-nine times out of a hundred the drudgery overrides any sense of delight in the task at hand, on that hundredth time, if we can bring some rhythm to bear on it (*heave*-ho, *lift*-pause, *left*-right), the thing feels different. It is subjected to a bigger thing, and becomes itself the occasion for expressing some rhythm that pulses in all of us.

So the function is transfigured by being subjected to a form, and when it has been subjected to that form, it is not clear which is governing which. To return to the "One foot up, one foot down", then: the experience of walking to town can be apprehended either as mere function (in which case it is hardly apprehended at all) or as a thing in itself. And it is to the thing itself that poetic language addresses itself, and the thing itself that is made visible in poetic language. That is, what would otherwise escape us is halted and addressed by poetic language. Or, more accurately, *we* are halted. It is as though poetry laid a hand on our arm and said, "Now steady. You are missing this in your prosaic dash past experience, and it is worth not missing." And so it focuses, say, on a walk to the city—not on the scenery or on the company or on the bustle round about, but on the activity itself, which might well be missed even if we were on a pleasure walk and were thinking about the lovely morning and the quaint villages through which we passed. What about this unnoticeable muscular means of propulsion? it asks. Is there anything here, in this tiny aspect of experience, worth contemplating? It is a humble function, this planting of one appendage on the road and then the other, ten thousand times over—hardly one of the profoundly and uniquely human acts that ought to occupy our attention. Any old millipede or monopod can *walk*. We scarcely distinguish ourselves here. But . . . "One foot up, one foot down, / That's the way to London town", left-right, left-right, heigh-ho, get-in-step, swing-it-along, keep-it-up, one foot up, one foot down. And we have to smile. For what was wholly unnoticeable because it was only useful has been illumined for us by this odd rhythmic spell, and for the first time in our lives we become aware of *walking* (as opposed even to going-for-a-walk, in which the center of attention is the scenery or the fresh air) as an experience in which there may be glory. And it had been done thus: our imagination has been hailed with a case in point, under the species of words, of what is also at work in walking—that is, rhythm—and, unless our imagination had been thus hailed, the chances of our having missed this particular awareness were pretty high.

This is part of the business of poetry, from the nursery rhyme to the *Divine Comedy*. It addresses our imagination and, with everything that is at its service, it tries to beguile us into the intense awareness of experience. It knows that our attention is cudgeled by functional concerns morning, noon, and night, and it suspects that this is not the desideratum. But it does not call us away from the "real" world of function into a garden of fancy that never existed anywhere. Rather, its high office is to ransom us from thrall to the deadly myth that life is cluttered and obstructed by necessity, and to return us to life with the awareness that it is packed with glory, and that the clutter of daily experience that we ordinarily apprehend as just that—clutter—may, on the contrary, be the epiphany of form—of the very order and harmony and serenity that we long for in our reveries. In order to bring this about, poetry may resort to the far away and long ago, or to the mythic or the heroic or the pastoral, but it does this in order to gain distance and hence perspective. It deplores the myopia that creeps through experience with no vision of the whole. It sees that the dismantling of experience by analysis may yield some view of its parts, but that it will never yield that sense of a perfect whole toward which imagination always strains.

The new myth would say, then, of poetry that what it achieves by dragooning and shaping common experience into something that seems to signal order and harmony and serenity, and hence joy, is a most rewarding fiction—the supreme fiction, perhaps. The old myth would say that it signals the supreme reality: the way things are.

Chapter Five

Sublimity, Soup Cans, Etc.

It may seem to be giving a disproportionate place to art to have a whole chapter on poetry and another on painting in a book that is not a book on aesthetics. But the particular way of looking at human experience which I am describing in this book is one which manifests itself in the poet's and painter's crafts. For in their work they bring to a sharp focus what all of us see more or less dimly all the time, anyway—that the formless wants a form; that raw matter wants to be shaped; that the invisible wants to become visible; that mere walking may be apprehended as a rhythmic and glorious thing; that the table wants setting for lunch; that an idea of royalty takes on shape in princes and borzois; that it is by the clothing of an idea in the vividness of form (either concrete or ritual) that it appears as significant.

Now this runs us back to the problem cited in the first chapter: that this is a world from which significance seems to have disappeared. At least the myth sovereign in our epoch will have it so. Things don't *mean* anything; they simply are, and the effort to keep significance alive is nostalgia or atavism. And, ironically, this disappearance of significance is the main burden of nearly all twentieth-century painting and poetry and drama. The old order, with Beatitude at the top and Hell at the bottom, and all things ranged and arrayed in between, has evaporated with the advent of science, goes the supposition. Hence we are lost. Alienated. Disfranchised. Forlorn. The stuff of our world and our experience suggests not a pattern of glory, but nothing at all. From these shards we must try to reconstruct something—a new pattern, a pattern with Man for a maker, since the old Maker has perished like the Titans, a pattern that will exhibit our awareness of forlornness and meaninglessness, and that will evince the courage, modesty, and bitterness appropriate to such creatures as we find ourselves to be. It may be possible, by looking at two painters, one from a period in which the old myth prevailed and one from the new, to see how these myths affect a man's way of seeing the world. On the one hand, we may get some idea of the kind of world in which ordinary things furnish the raw matter from which imagination can shape a vision of luminescence and sublimity; and on the other, we may see the kind of world in which no such vision is possible.

The two men in question here are the seventeenth-century Fleming Vermeer and the twentieth-century American Warhol. Their works exhibit a piquant contrast when placed side by side. Both men paint with scrupulous attention to the way things look to us, as opposed, say, to painters who try by manipulating their materials in curious ways to renew our ability to see things, or who leave the realm of familiar objects altogether.

To a casual eye, there is a great similarity of technique between the two. In an epoch when we find ourselves standing in muttering uncertainty in front of canvases, wondering what questions we may ask, or whether perhaps the very inclination to *ask* questions does not betray a touching rusticity on our part—in such an epoch, it is a relief to come upon a canvas that holds a picture *of* something. Aha, we say, I know what *this* is. It is a girl sitting at a table next to a window, talking to a dashing gentleman. And this one here, it is quite unmistakably—a *soup can*! Now what can the man have meant?

And there it is. With the Vermeer we do not find ourselves asking right away what it means. The question of meaning hardly seems necessary as we contemplate the serene perfection of the colors—the gentleman's wonderful red coat and black hat, and the girl's blue gown and alabaster skin, and the light coming in from the window high on the wall. There is nothing in the least astonishing here. Just two people sitting at a table in the corner of a room. No heroics. No martyrdom. No angelic annunciation. No grandees. Not, really, very auspicious subject matter for a painting. But, we suspect, everything is here. Perhaps this is what is implicit also in all heroics and martyrdoms and annunciations: two people facing each other. A man and a woman. And from this common stuff there arise all the motions and energies that mark human existence and that move history. Every myth and legend and all the tales of faerie, and all dramas and dreams and reveries evoke something like this. And even if we are not adroit critics of painting and cannot comment intelligently on the technique, yet we find ourselves beguiled by it. Here is something we understand. Here is something that pleases us. And here is something that arouses in us, if we allow ourselves the austere luxury of contemplation, the awareness of luminescence and sublimity. From this simple matrix, Vermeer has formed something that both suggests, and is itself an instance of, perfection. He did not travel to Xanadu or Ultima Thule to find it. He went into the next room. He did not invoke goddesses or emperors or dryads to figure it for us. He looked around him.

But hanging next to it here (if we can fancy a gallery that would juxtapose these two gentlemen) is Mr. Warhol's soup can. Isn't this, though, a natural juxtaposition? In the other rooms of the gallery there are wild smudgings and dribbles, or grotesquely tumescent or angular figures, or regal portraits, or nude warriors. Here in this room we have grouped together paintings that are, for a start, taken from everyday life, and then treated with painstaking accuracy so that they look like what they are supposed to look like. We might hang a photograph in here, too.

But this soup can. It seems a banality, if not an obscenity, next to this Vermeer. If he is going to turn our attention to food at all, couldn't the artist have chosen an oil cruet, perhaps, or a pepper mill, or at least a Chianti bottle? Something with an interesting shape, and some texture, that would evoke for us the world of fine cuisine? Why this stark commercialism? We come to the gallery to get *away* from the A&P. After all, we are in there almost every morning of our lives. It is a bore to be hailed by a large and intransigent soup can here. It is slightly jolting, most certainly depressing, and, after a bit, alarming. The initial cackle of amusement flickers off into the quavering heh-hehs of the man who finds that the funny person in the mask is the executioner after all.

But the soup can is common life, just like the Vermeer. It is undistorted, just like the Vermeer. It is not possible superficially to find much difference between the two paintings. Both artists are excellent craftsmen; both focus on common things; both treat these things with no apparent distortion. Is there, then, any special difference between the visions of these two painters? And if so, is it important?

It would be hard to find anyone who would argue that there is no difference between Vermeer and Warhol. Since this is not a book of art criticism, I shall leave it to others better qualified than I to point out the technical differences. What is important here is the matter of sensibility.

Sensibility is an elusive matter, and it is a word that one thinks of more in connection with the eighteenth century than with our own, since it was a popular word then. It denotes something like the consciousness, the frame of mind, of a given era, but not exactly these. It has to do with taste, too. It arises eventually from the whole pool of presuppositions that lies at the bottom of everything that contributes to the era, and that nourishes the particular set of responses to experience that marks the era.

It is visible in a thousand different ways: the literature, the architecture, the dress, the humor, the dance, the politics, the amusements—all these register the sensibility of the time. For instance, something of the difference between the age of Pericles and that of Louis XVI can be seen by comparing the buildings put up in each. The differences here are not primarily engineering matters of how best to hold up a roof. By the same token, the architects of the twelfth century and

Frank Lloyd Wright would agree on various fundamental matters of stress and materials and so on, but when they set to building you get on the one hand Chartres, and on the other the Guggenheim Museum. Similarly, if you compare the jokes and parlor games that made our grandparents shriek with laughter with the kinds of humor that mark our own time, you are up against a matter of sensibility. Why do we writhe in embarrassment over their puns and conundrums? And why do we find various forms of the macabre and the banal funny? Or again, why did our forebears do the gavotte and we the frug? Or what is it about a poster of a stern Uncle Sam pointing his finger and wanting "*You!*" that appeals to one generation and about a poster of Allen Ginsberg costumed in grotesque parody of that same Uncle Sam that appeals to another generation? It is a matter of sensibility.

The painting of a given era is one of the indexes of its sensibility. This is not to say that the painters simply offer us charts by which we may locate the contemporary imagination. Indeed, it has often been the case, and especially since about 1850, that the painters wish to be on record as ferociously disavowing the contemporary sensibility. But then you get a disjuncture that raises the question as to who *does* represent the sensibility of the epoch: Picasso or Madison Avenue? But even granting the quarrel which the artists of the last hundred years have carried on with their epoch, there is still a sense in which it can be said that the painting in that period bespeaks the sensibility as much as Detroit and Hollywood do.

For both sets of phenomena (the art or the mass vulgarity) represent attempts to come to terms with a

world that has been in effect re-created since the Enlightenment. It is a re-creation that is analogous to
that original creation described in old Scriptures, in
that both creations involve the drawing into form of
something by means of *articulation*. This process was
understood in the old tales as having been accom-
plished by a creative energy known as the Word. It
was by the Word (the Word of God, it was) that the
heavens and earth were shaped into the system seen by
men in the ages known to us as the ages of belief. The
implication was that by *utterance* you get something
that did not exist before the utterance. The system
that was articulated in that original creative event was
ordered (God or the gods at the top, and the rest of
us—archangels, men, clams—ranged down the ladder), significant (things *meant* something; the common
stuff of experience signaled something that was true
all up and down the ladder), and teleological (that is,
purposive: the ladder *went* somewhere).

The re-creation which took place in Western history
involved a dismantling of that ordered, significant,
and purposive world. It does not much matter
whether your view of that re-creation is pro or con;
your understanding of it will be about the same.
Briefly (and this is in all schoolbooks), it is this: it
came about that there arose ways of looking at and
describing things other than by attributing them to
the gods. The method seemed fair enough: just look *at*
something and see if you can, without commandeer-
ing all the hosts of heaven, discover how it works. See
if you can, by observing many instances of a given
kind of behavior, discern a pattern and articulate it.

The men who began this sort of thing were by no means engaged in an assault on what they and the whole world before them had been taught to think about things. They were doing what the human mind is supposed to do, that is, asking questions. Their method was analytic, in that it approached things as sums of parts (a tree is, really, so much carbon and hydrogen and oxygen). And it was empirical in that it refused to rise higher than the data at hand forced it to rise, so that you may say that rocks in fact fall, but that there is nothing in the falling action that forces the idea of a jinni who makes it fall.

The world that emerged from the effort had very little in common with the first world. This analytic scrutiny of data at first seemed to yield a world still ordered, and so you had an eighteenth century rejoicing in the neatness which is observable in everything, trimming its hedges and plotting its garden paths into severe designs, and singing to God (the deist god, that is, not the threatening theist one) about how right it is to have the rich man in his castle and the poor man at his gate. But the method, pressed further, began to undermine these nice ideas, and some brave spirits were so exhilarated with the possibilities of the new creation that they called it all the Enlightenment. The notion of any divinely sanctioned order evaporated, of course (you don't, no matter how hard you try, conjure a god from crystalline structure)—and, within 150 years, the notion of any order. And so there is, in our own century, the irony of an era that sees itself as having "come of age" (a rather patronizing view of other centuries), but which is at the same time hysterically aware of the impossibility of making any affirmations whatever.

The dogmas of the new myth have been written into the books and clamped into the archives of modern imagination as securely as the Holy Bible was ever chained by the good abbot to the desk in the monastery library. And precisely as there were questions then which, if you asked them, put you in peril of thumbscrews, so there are questions now which are not to be asked, on pain of more subtle thumbscrews—ostracism, or an avuncular pat on the head and the suggestion that you get busy reading your modern psychology, history, and sociology.

It is, for instance, held to be anachronistic to press the question of *meaning*. We have moved out into a region where that question will not get us anywhere, it is held, since we have long since learned to live with the absence of meaning. We have learned this since our method of exploring and describing our world has not yielded anything that can be called meaning. The category is, then, irrelevant, despite the fact that we must struggle from time to time with a pestiferous wistfulness that keeps insisting that we *would* like to ask the question. Similarly, we may ask questions about self-knowledge, but not about the Beatific Vision, since advanced research has uncovered a great deal about the former, but nothing about the latter. It is not a fruitful category.

There lies, then, at the bottom of modern discussion an array of suppositions that are held to be axiomatic. It is a post-Enlightenment array, and issues in an ironic simultaneity of omniscience and agnosticism; that is, that we, unlike any other epoch in history, finally have the equipment to conquer the unknown, but that at the same time we strenuously disavow the assumption that a man can really know anything at all about what is at stake in existence.

From this array of suppositions there derives the sensibility of our epoch, just as the sensibility of the seventeenth century was traceable to its ideas about cosmic order, or of the ninth to *its* ideas about cosmic order. That is, where other ages saw man as a paragon and spoke of Adam and Achilles, ours sees him as a chemical excrescence, and hence speaks of Willy Loman and Jake Barnes. For the same reason, we do not see the figures of Beowulf and Roland as very timely images. And because we do not understand man as being addressed by the god, we do not find many annunciations being depicted by our painters. And since our new creation is a wasteland populated by yahoos and churls, that is what we must celebrate in our imagery. Our sensibility, in other words, derives from our presuppositions about the nature of things.

To get back to Vermeer and Warhol, then. Both of them looked at the things at hand. Vermeer lived in an age when it was possible to do so and see luminescence and sublimity. Whereas former centuries had evoked that sublimity by means of an incandescent religious imagery (angels, bishops, saints, virgins), Vermeer saw it at hand. His century was one that was intensely conscious of common experience, and that turned to it rather than to heroics and hagiology for its imagery. The painters painted kitchens and farmyards and dirt roads and oxen—that is, the stuff of common experience—but there was no degradation implied. These things were seen as fruitful sources for a noble imagery. There were implicit in the kitchen or the farmyard not boredom and thralldom and ignominy, but order and equanimity and the great, given rhythms of experience in which a man participates to his ennobling.

Warhol, on the other hand, paints in an age whose sensibility is different from this. Its researches have convinced it that there are indeed boredom and thralldom and ignominy, and that luminescence and sublimity belong only to ages that fled to *belief* for meanings in things. The re-created world, formed according to the analytic Word, is a world without form, and void, and darkness is upon the face of the Enlightenment, and it is only some sinister pterodactyl and not the Holy Ghost that broods over the deep.

The experience of fragmentation has shaped the sensibility of our epoch. When it began to dawn on the Western mind that it had, in fact, succeeded in dismantling things, fright and vexation beset men. The nineteenth century is full of spirits trying bravely to find some basis for reconstruction (Arnold, Newman, Emerson, Mill, Browning, Tennyson). As time wore on, the vexation turned to bitterness and frustration (Hardy). Since there was no longer any point in focusing on any cosmic order (there was none), the locale of inquiry was shifted to what was inside our consciousness (Freud, Joyce, Lawrence, the surrealists). Since the idea of things as images of anything—that is, as having any significant *content*—had ebbed with the old myth, the artist's concern came to be with *form*— with the effort to manipulate his materials in various ways in order to discover aesthetically (and, it was hoped, spiritually) satisfying patterns, since the old possibilities of satisfaction had disappeared. Hence, in all the arts, the questions raised were formal ones. In the novel, for instance, Joyce and James and Conrad and Virginia Woolf brought the craft to a highly self-conscious state, in which the preeminent concern was with structure. Similarly, in painting it was formal questions that gave rise to abstraction and cubism and expressionism. In philosophy the inquiry turned away from metaphysics to language, which is to say, to the formal question of how meaning may or may not yield itself to symbolic utterance. In the behavioral and social sciences, the concern came to be with the form of things, so that the focus of study is, for instance, upon guilt *feelings* rather than upon the question of actual guilt.

Then suddenly, into this finely wrought state of affairs there drops Mr. Warhol and his soup cans and stacks of scouring-pad boxes. It looks for a moment like pure, unapologetic content. No ambiguity, no elusiveness, no subtlety, just the terrifying confrontation with the brutal concrete. We experience this as a jolt in that our attention has, for fifty years, been honed to a fine state of receptivity to questions of *form*, and now, when we are hailed by those blatant *things*, we hardly know what to do about it. We may respond with disgust, or with blankness, or with applause (this is called "camp", and denotes a frame of mind that laughs brightly at its own clumsiness when it barks its shins stumbling along the corridor to the gibbet).

The sensibility which is apparent in the Warhol painting suggests two things. It is, for one thing, a sensibility that is aware of a radical fragmentation of experience, and it utters that awareness by isolating chunks of experience (we all open soup cans from time to time) and exhibiting them for contemplation. But where the Vermeer painting suggests the isolated experience as a paradigm of perfection, the Warhol suggests an unnerving banality: Is *this* what our life is about, when all the time we thought we were something noble? And, secondly, it is a sensibility that is the child of the divorce of form and content, or at least of the disappearance of any *finally* significant content from the data of our experience, since under the new myth the only final reality is a blank, and hence the stuff of the world and of our experience (trees and sex and color and courage) cannot be seen as the forms under which the eternal appears. Or, put another way, they cannot be seen as images of the eternal (the way things are, that is), since "the eternal" is no longer seen as designating anything that really does lie behind the stuff of the world.

Hence the task of the painter is thrown into a different light from that in which it was understood during the ages when things *were* seen as images of the eternal. Then the artist manipulated his materials in an effort to gain an aesthetic repose—the repose that attends the spectacle of balance and symmetry and appropriateness and harmony, and the perfect union of form and content, so that the thing achieved did not appear to be an idea plus shape (grief plus stone in the *Pietà*, or rage plus rhythm in the *Iliad*). The end sought was a thing in which there could be no separating form and content, but rather the sense that from the marble formed thus, or from the poetry, there proceeded a single vision.

And the artist under the old myth could see this kind of activity as making perfect sense because what he was doing was enacting and participating in the way things were anyway. His world *was* an image of the eternal; that is, it was a pattern of appearances organized and shaped by the eternal Word to exhibit the pattern of the eternal. Hence his response to this kind of world was to create things that would, under their own modes (stone, words, paint), exhibit that pattern. This is not to say that every artist had a religious animus. It is only to point out that imagination was at home in such a world, since what it was always doing anyway (making images and seeing correspondences and shaping experience) was wholly appropriate in that kind of world.

But of course there had to be an agonizing reappraisal of all that sort of thing when it was discovered that the world was no such place, and that it was only primitive hopefulness that made men suppose it was. Hence the artist had a rather different task. He could not disavow the urge toward aesthetic repose, any more than he could disavow hunger or fatigue or sexual appetite. It is one of the things that is *there*. So he had to admit that he was animated by the same energy as his predecessors under the old myth, but he could declare his independence. That is, since there was no real connection between his imagination and the nature of the world outside him, he could turn the activities of his imagination toward the exploration of new and independent bases for aesthetic satisfaction—bases that had nothing to do with the way things really might be, since that is unknowable, and probably random in any case. In other words, artists became, in one sense, metaphysicians, probing the possibilities of aesthetic satisfaction in new materials and techniques. Hence the experiments with "found objects" and abstraction and images from the subconscious, and the effort to prod us toward new visual experiences. And hence the metaphysical ring in the comments which most twentieth-century painters make about their own work. Theirs is a heavy task indeed. Whereas their forebears could evoke and celebrate a world in which the appearance of things answered to the nature of things, and hence furnished rich materials for the imagination, these men have to find some source for aesthetic satisfaction other than this fortunate correspondence. Hence also the overwhelming sense of experiment and exploration in modern painting and sculpture. We haven't yet found an agreed-upon source from which we can draw images of affirmation. (It must be said for the artists of the twentieth century that theirs has been one of the most varied, powerful, and dazzling outputs of any period of art. The very ambiguities and questions of the epoch have goaded them in their promethean task, and their response is a record of human courage, passion, and resourcefulness.)

The soup can, then. It is one of a vast number of twentieth-century attempts to find this thing, or that thing, as a possible step toward aesthetic satisfaction. In this case it is by singling out for an implacable look an item from everyone's daily experience, and manipulating it in order to gain the maximum sense of intransigence, the idea being, I should think, that we will try *this*, then (instead of abstraction or surrealism or cubism) as an aesthetic foray. And these comments would apply whether or not the artist is pulling the public's leg, which is very pertinent question in the case of Mr. Warhol. But whether he is doing this or not, his work—or let us call it his hoax—has an effect on us such that its consequences are the same as they would be if he were dead serious. In other words, his work here may be an instance of "camp", but it nonetheless derives its particular *effect* from either being, or posing as, what it appears to us to be. It is as though the artist were saying: Right, the artist's material is the common stuff of experience. *This* is the common stuff of *your* experience, O twentieth century. Soup cans. Not soup cans romanticized, or soup cans abstracted, or soup cans gilded. Just large intransigent cans. How about that for your art? We've got to come to terms with the brutal actualities of life—a soup can is a soup can is a soup can, and not Saint Michael and all angels, as other epochs thought it might be.

Chapter Six

Autocrats,
Autonomy, and Acorns

But it is not a mere aesthetic shift that has occurred from the old to the new myth. That would be interesting enough, and food for long, taxing discussions. The shift has also redefined for us the way we think about what we are supposed to *do*, and the rationale we find for our attitudes and actions. It redefines, in other words, the moral question.

It can always be asked of a viewpoint what *difference* it makes. There are a thousand intriguing ideas (matter is a figment of somebody's imagination; we are reincarnated incessantly; the moon is made of green cheese) that bid for our attention (and always win someone's) whose effects are hard to trace in any practical way. We feel patronizing toward an idea that does nothing but call attention to itself and results in a group whose activity is a whispered and initiated sharing of "our" truth. To a certain extent, of course, this is inevitable; the most exalted and substantial ideas have this in common with the most ragtag and bobtail inventions, that they attract groups to themselves and become a center of focus, talk, and ritual. So that the Holy Synod of Russian Orthodoxy, the Americans for Democratic Action, the Ku Klux Klan, the local witchcraft society, the communist cell, and the Scientific Humanism study group may all be lumped together, according to one kind of analysis, as merely people drawn together by some common idea, seeing themselves as a group of illuminati and outsiders as more or less benighted. And, as long as they do nothing but talk to themselves about their ideas, and celebrate those ideas inside their temples, the rest of us don't much mind one way or another. It is only when Marxism finally throws out tsarism, or when the witches hex our children, or Christians give us a cup of cold water, that we take any notice.

If four hundred years ago we had chanced upon a small group of intellectuals chatting excitedly over their ale about the idea that the proper study of mankind is man, and that the way to carry on that study is to rule out from the start all mythic and superstitious presuppositions and to lay down strict rules as to what may and may not be admitted into serious discussion ("facts", yes; prophecies, omens, and angels, no)—if we had come across this, we would undoubtedly have tried to arrange a public burning. If we had been astute enough, we would have argued that that sort of talk could lead only to the eventual view that there *was* in fact nothing but these "facts" to be talked about, and that all our angels and gods and terrors would vanish, and what a perdition that would be for us all. Let us stamp out the evil now! Let us have these heretics to the stake at once!

And, while our method of countering the threat would have been a bit robust, our idea would have been quite correct: the angels and gods and terrors and glories *did* vanish, and men did take a drastically different view of things than they had in the old ages when sibyls and priests told them that the gods were very much concerned with human affairs and were likely to intervene if men didn't behave properly.

In any case, the emancipation of human imagination from this old idea that men—we and the stars and acorns and angels—are all operating in our different modes under the sovereignty of the whole pattern (it was sometimes called the Dance, as though we were all moving solemnly and joyously in a measure, finding our true freedom in the discovery of the steps appointed to us)—the emancipation from this idea resulted eventually, of course, in a radical change in our whole idea of what it means to be free. Whereas heretofore the idea of human freedom was understood as in some way analogous to, say, Shakespeare's "freedom" to operate within the confines of a sonnet and come up with something approximating perfection, or the acorn's "freedom" to develop according to the austerely limited possibilities of its own being into an enormous oak, or the athlete's "freedom" to execute a breathtaking jump by virtue of having subjected himself to a harsh regimen, now the idea of freedom involved something more like autonomy. That is, the whole consciousness of human life as appearing *under* some cosmic aegis disappeared with the failure of the new myth to uncover any angels, unicorns, or other messengers from the court. And, if we can't see it, it's not there—or at least we'll proceed on that assumption until we stumble upon it; so said the new myth. And lo, nothing has been stumbled upon yet. No angel has whirled up from anyone's test tube like the jinni from an Eastern lamp. Therefore, says the new myth, according to the rules of the game, we disallow

all those unverifiable ideas that undergirded and energized the old myth. It is simply not clear (in *our*
lenses, at any rate) that there is anything to be taken
seriously about all that, and so we must get on with
it, and let whatever emerges emerge.

Obviously, with the receding and evaporating of the
angels and devils, the idea as to the nature of human
life changes. We are alone! This is the most astonishing and exhilarating of the dicta that proceed from the
new myth. No one is looking over our shoulder. Neither Osiris nor Yahweh nor Zeus nor Wotan will tax
us with inquiries as to what we are doing. We are not
under anyone's aegis. We owe fealty to no one but
ourselves.

Hence, we announce our own liberation. It is a liberation from aeons of tyranny—the tyranny of superstition and fear and obligation and code. We will grow
into our own role as man exactly to the extent that we
assume the burden hitherto borne by the god—the
burden of pointing out the pattern, of indicating what
is good and lasting and worthy in contrast to what is
evil and ephemeral and worthless. We announce, that
is, our autonomy.

The idea of autonomy is a bracing one. It brings
with it a whole imagery of independence, and of new
worlds to conquer, and of risk and courage and
progress, and above all, self-determination. The release from servitude to deities and their vicars set man
free, we are told, to conquer his own world and re-
fashion it according to the light shed on it by the new
myth. The political, intellectual, and moral effects of
it all are common knowledge, for they are the stuff of
which the modern world is made. It is not mere coin-

cidence that kings and their divine right fled as the community of man thought of itself as bound together not by fealty to the royal figure, but by its common involvement in the business of being human. The political imagery changed, that is, from hierarchy to the ad hoc committee, from fiat to consensus, from arbitrariness to arbitration, from autocracy to participation. By the same token, it is not coincidence that, with the receding of the old myth, the suzerainty of theology among the intellectual disciplines should have been supplanted by the physical and social and behavioral sciences. It's no use talking about what cannot possibly be verified, went the argument, when we have our hands full for several millennia with the agenda of things that *can* be verified. Never mind who the god of the wood is; let's find out what this tree is *made* of. It's all very well to talk of blood as a propitiatory elixir, but that line of thought never discovered plasma, which is what this wounded soldier needs at this point. The intellectual images shifted, in the process, from creators and animation and personification (Atlas versus gravity, for example) to hap and mechanism and abstraction.

By the same token again, the cry "freedom!"— which is an ancient human cry—has one set of images associated with it to the mind that sees everything under somebody's aegis, and another set to the mind that sees man to be autonomous. There has always, of course, been the cry of the human imagination against the outrages of power, and this would be common to all men, under whatever myth. Presumably, the slaves under Caesar, and the muzhiks under Ivan the Terrible, and the Czechs under Stalin would all share some sense of oppression, regardless of whether or not their myths told them that some men were *supposed*, in the cosmic pattern, to be almighty and others to be miserable. We would all rather not be *forced* into fealty. And, under the new myth, fealty itself is a grating idea that drags up specters either of sycophantic courtiers bobbing about the throne, or of humpbacked clouts flogged into animal servitude by draconian overseers. It is natural that, with the disappearance of divine sanctions for authority, the notion of authority itself should come under surveillance, since the question of an origin for authority is thrown open. It was possible for a while, of course, to supplant the god with the idea of tradition, or history or consensus, as sources for authority, but the very nature of the new myth, since it rises from the notion of autonomy, is to tend toward the idea of autonomy in all regions. In the political confrontation occurring in America, it is becoming clear to us how difficult it is to insist on any binding rationale at all for political authority. The *gods* are certainly dead—that part at least is settled; and *tradition* is a gorgon that must be slain; and *history* has been so botched that it must be begun anew by a generation that has been delivered from the sins and mistakes of its fathers; and consensus is only bourgeois tergiversation for power politics.

It is a bitter revelation to the generation that has worked so painstakingly over the last seventy-five years to build a liberal society on the foundation of the new myth to be told by the children whom it has nourished on that myth that the whole thing is sour. If, say these children, we really *are* autonomous as you have taught us, then we shall enjoy that autonomy.

You and your fathers worked to free yourselves from the autocratic hand of the gods and to build a secular order that would maintain itself by the mutual consent of its members. We do not consent to this order. You have made as horrible a mess of society as any priest-craft ever did, and we withhold consent. Your politics and morality are disgusting in their sluggishness and dullness. You are niggards to have declared your emancipation from superstition and autocracy only to allow the tyrannies of the old order to re-form themselves under new names in *your* order. Your crusty congresses and parliaments are no better than the medieval privy councils and diets. Your halfhearted morality is cynical in that it pays lip service to autonomy, all the while perpetuating the strictures of the old order. So, just as you built your order on the ashes of the old, we will burn your order and build an authentically new one, in which for the first time in human history genuine freedom will be manifest. Police, power structures, prejudice, cupidity—these will have disappeared. Men will enjoy in actuality the autonomy that has been announced in their theories.

In the moral as in the political realm, freedom suggests to this mind the right of the individual to make his own choices on the basis of private criteria. The individual is placed at the center of the moral question: he himself is the measure of what he will do, and he himself is the judge. His fealty is to his own inclinations. A popular slogan of this mind is "doing your own thing"—the idea being that the only judge of your action is your own decision to *do* it. This places the Salvation Army girl, the sodomite, the American

Legion conventioneer, the dope pusher, Castro, and Duvalier on an exact par: each of them is doing his own thing. The man who takes this view cannot accept the sovereignty of the gods, of tradition, of history, or of consensus. He experiences directly and forcefully the sovereignty of his own passions (curiosity, appetite, revenge, etc.), and it is to these that he gives fealty. The imagery becomes one, then, of spontaneity and directness and earthiness: do your own thing, man, do your own thing.

It is perhaps above all astonishing to note that the great emancipation of the human spirit from the dread placed upon it by superstition and priestcraft released not a blithe and merry spirit capering out over the fields of a new world unhaunted by the goblins and angels, but a dread more ravaging than all of them, the dread described by modern prophets as *angst*. It was *angst* that leaped upon man's back when the incubi had been exorcised. When the exorcism had driven the last of the horrors away, and when the iconography of hell, and of souls in torment, and of judgments and sacrifices and wrath, was no longer felt to be relevant, there came an iconography of ennui and disgust and anguish. The burden, when it fell from the shoulders of Atlas onto our own, was found to be too heavy.

The awareness of what autonomy means to us has been uttered ten thousand times in our fiction and drama, and it has been analyzed in a hundred shelves of essays. We must cope with the simultaneous discovery that we are *not* the center either of attention or of geography in the universe, but that we *are* the center of attention for ourselves, and the only measure of values.

There is no word from the universe to tell us what to do. There is no clue, by way of Scripture or analogy or visitation, to tell us what, in fact, the rules are.

There is a sense, then, in which the burden assumed by autonomous man is the burden of freedom, and the kind of freedom looked for by the autonomous mind is one that is one thing in the anticipation and another in the having. In anticipation, it looks like the breaking free of all the trammels and weights that have borne us down to the ground since the beginning of history, and the gate to a new and unexampled liberty. It is the freedom that is imagined by the anarchic point of view, and that attributes man's ills to the tangle of chains that had held him down like some butterfly enmeshed in a cobweb.

But when it is won, what? It has never, of course, been quite won. But when it has been won as much as we have done, what does it look like?

It looks like a bleak business, if the reading given to the situation by our poets, dramatists, and filmmakers is to be credited at all. For, to our chagrin, we discover that the declaration of autonomy has issued not in a race of free, masterly men, but rather in a race that can be described by its poets and dramatists only as bored, vexed, frantic, embittered, and sniffling. It would have helped, of course, if the idea that man under the old myth was denied his full nobility to the extent that he saw himself as *under* someone's authority—if that idea could have been supported by the poets and dramatists from those ages. But, unhappily for the new myth, that is not how it appears. For the figure of man, no matter how harassed, how assaulted, how outraged, drawn by those poets was not of man crushed. In the extremity of rage, disenchantment, or disgust, that figure never lost its nobility. Achilles, raging about having been cheated, was still Achilles, a figure who will stand until the end of human time as the figure of a strong man. Indeed, that strength was not gained primarily by his conquests in battle. That part is assumed about him in Homer's portrait. It was, rather, in his response to difficult situations that he becomes the figure that he is in our eyes. Similarly Lear, for all his foolishness, stands to us as an image of a noble spirit wracked by circumstances brought upon itself by that very foolishness, crying, "Howl, Howl, Howl, Howl!" and yet in that very cry evincing a strength—at least the strength to howl and not snivel. Likewise Hamlet, certainly a spirit congenial to modern man, torn by whatever it was that was tearing him—disgust or impotence or hesitation—found the whole world "weary, stale, flat, and unprofitable". He never howled. His response was quite different from Lear's. But, however it manifested itself, his response to his experience never exhibited him as a crawling, weak thing. Likewise the figure of Beowulf, who certainly was no stranger to terror and discouragement. He had his faults, but in his fights with the monster Grendel, and Grendel's mother, and with the dragon, his spirit was the spirit of a strong creature and not a weakling. These are the figures of man given us by the old myth—the myth that man is addressed by something that asks his fealty, that he exists under the aegis of the god.

But the autonomous man, on his breezy eminence, does not look like this. He looks like Arthur Miller's salesman Willy Loman. He looks like Hemingway's emasculated Jake Barnes. Or he looks jaded, perplexed blasé, damned.

Federico Fellini has given us a vivid imagery of boredom which we have had to hail as *true*. Ingmar Bergman has harried us with his images of vacuity, ambiguity, and perplexity. Eugene Ionesco has given us images of people with no resources at all to bring to an absurdity like rhinoceroses running about the streets. Jean Luc Godard, in *Weekend*, has strung together an outrageous parable of people confronted with the grotesque and fragmented (literally: the film is full of dismembered corpses; and dramatically: the sequence of events becomes more and more random) and able to bring no response whatever to it all. It is not even clear where the threshold of reality lies for them, in that they begin to register an awareness that they are only acting in a French film. Michelangelo Antonioni has raised similar questions in his popular *Blow-up*, in that, after a long sequence of rather random events (a young London photographer, whose own domestic modus vivendi is exhilaratingly random, wanders in and out of an antique shop and through a park, spots an obviously huggermugger romantic liaison, then a corpse, can't get anyone aroused about the corpse and doesn't think to summon the law)—after this, the hero encounters a group of tatterdemalion wags, who have periodically driven on and off screen, playing a game of nontennis: no court, no rackets, no net, no ball, but a rousing game nonetheless. The hero contemplates this, bemused, and then, when the nonball is accidentally hit off the noncourt, he runs and picks it up and throws it back to the players. He has concluded that since "reality" is so ambiguous anyway, we may as well abandon the effort to distinguish it from illusion.

A film which attracted enormous attention when it came out in the latter 1960s, although it is not good drama, is Mike Nichols' *The Graduate*. Here again, it is possible to see the kind of consciousness that derives from the declaration of autonomy, and the idea that nothing means anything. The hero, sensitive, questing, intelligent, harmless, finds himself caught in the disgusting and banal habitat of swimming pools, cocktails, and high-octane opulence that his parents and their friends have made for themselves. The imagery bludgeons us as it does him with the futility and horror of it all. He is seduced by one of his parents' contemporaries, then falls in love with her daughter. The drama is thin, in that by the end of the film not only have the questions raised in the action not been settled (you can have a very good drama that doesn't *settle* the questions); they have been lost track of. But, more fundamentally than that, it eventually dawns upon the viewer that here is a course of action carried on not with aggressive "immoral" intentions, but quite simply without any reference whatever to the codes and taboos that cramped human activity under the old myth. It follows, as the night the day, that autonomous man must make his own choices about things without the tutelage of these codes. Hence, the only thing energizing the action in *The Graduate* is inclination. Or, to grant the film a bit more substance, romantic passion. The boy *loves* the girl. Now this, of course, is to say everything, and to place the drama for a moment on a tentative level with the stories of Troilus, Tristan, Lancelot, and the rest. The difficulty

with this equation is, however, that under the old
myth (that we are all subject to the demands of the
pattern), while the dramas were about human passion
and adultery and jiggery-pokery, and everyone's efforts to skirt the demands of the pattern (e.g., Lancelot and Guinevere knew perfectly well what adultery
was, but they loved each other so much that they
found themselves caught in the tragic and lifelong necessity of dodging what they believed to be true)—
while the dramas were about the same subject matter
as *The Graduate*, there was implicit in the conflict
which energized them the precise awareness of the discrepancy between what the heroes *were*, in fact, doing,
and what they ought to have done. But in *The Graduate*, there is not the shadow of recognition *on the part of
the drama as a whole* of such a discrepancy. The mother,
the boy's first lover, stung by jealousy and the hint of
her own inadequacy to satisfy him forever, forbids him
ever to see her daughter. There is the suggestion here
that she doesn't want her daughter to be the sort of
woman she herself is, and this suggestion raises, of
course, moral questions: Why *not*? What is it about
this particular *kind* of experience that makes you want
to protect your daughter from it, whereas presumably
you would not mind if she had a sandwich with the
boy? But, while the mother may have some such re-
sidual feelings, there is no recognition of this kind of
thing in the drama as a whole. The viewer is drawn
into a climate in which he finds himself all unawares
applauding wildly over events that have a certain
magic about them, but which leave not only unan-
swered but *unasked* all the questions that are implied in
the preceding events. The drama unfolds and then

folds again entirely without reference to *moral* questions—and we find ourselves applauding.

Perhaps the most drastic of the contemporary celebrations of autonomy in cinema are the films of Andy Warhol. Here there is no *awareness* of perdition, as there is in Bergman, that is, no vexation of the human mind contemplating alienation and ambiguity. Nor is there the icy edge of Fellini or Antonioni, whose images of sophisticated perdition have arrested us all. Much less is there the terror or sorrow or confusion displayed for us by Godard, Buñuel, or Truffaut. There is, rather, the mild, amiable, and languorous celebration of life lived without any consciousness of moral conflict. As one watches a Warhol film, he finds himself beguiled into a world where his moral questions seem odd, gratuitous, even childish. These people have got rid of the clutter in life. They are right where it's at. There are no brittle and flimsy *conventions* governing their relationships. One minute follows the next with random immediacy, untangled by skeins dragged in from heaven, history, or even the hour before. Clothes, along with conventions of all sorts, are irrelevant. There is no brisk nudist doctrine ("Come, we're better off without clothes; let's have them off so we can be ourselves") any more than there is a doctrine of anything else. It is simply that clothes and schedules and vows and conventions are neither here nor there. Unlike Lancelot and Guinevere's situation, for instance, there is no *conflict* aroused by random cohabitation. Visit your friends, leave your clothes on or have them off, read a magazine, cohabit, chat, whatever—there are no *teeth* in any action or relationship. In one of Warhol's films, the hero, a boy who is married and has an infant child, earns the daily bread by functioning as a male whore. In reply to one of his brief partners who asks him about his wife, he says with a certain amount of patient exasperation and incredulity, "She knows where I'm at, man, she knows where I'm at." He comes home to find his wife on the bed with a (female) lover, and his response is to crawl onto the bed, allow them to pull his clothes off, then drop off to sleep as they carry on in each other's arms. In this and in many of Warhol's films, there is, as I say, the mild, amiable, and languorous celebration of life as it might be lived without "hangups"—hang-ups being our hysterical preoccupation with things like fidelity and continence and focus. Warhol's camera is the eye that sees things thus. It sits on its tripod like an unblinking toad, registering absolutely nothing about a given situation. Just as in one film a transvestite and a lesbian sit on a couch thumbing idly through a movie magazine and registering nothing while six feet away an extremely bizarre sexual exchange is occurring, so Warhol's camera gazes dispassionately, with neither glee nor scandal, at every variety of behavior.

But no. Not every variety. There are no acts of courage. No acts of generosity. No acts of sacrifice or loyalty. No delight and laughter. No pain or grief. No torment and endurance and desolation. Only the murmur of creatures untroubled by the hard distinctions and choices that human beings have to make. In an ironic way, the declaration of autonomy (from everything) has brought the situation full circle to what the new myth would insist obtained under the old, that is, to the serfdom in which no choices are possible. For, just as the absolute *lack* of option for a slave building the pyramid was the quality of his being a slave, so the absolute openness of option for the Warhol character is a form of slavery. Except that this time the taskmaster is ennui. It may be that if Warhol's name is placed among the great artists of history, it will be as the one who succeeded, as no one else ever did, in finding images of tyrannic ennui. For the inhabitants of the Warhol world have lost the options of renunciation and joy and sweat and pain and tears and fulfillment. The shackles that they have broken are shackles like highway signs and yellow lines and gravity and fatigue and conscience—all the things that drastically limit the choices for the rest of us, and that crowd us along and force us to do *this* and not *that* time after time.

For it is in these limitations that the old myth found the definition of freedom. Whatever freedom was, it was to be found, ironically, via the strait gate. It was thought of not as a matter of self-determination but rather as a matter of the capacity to experience one's own perfection as joy. The question for Adam and Eve was not that they enjoy a realm in which no strictures existed: it was, rather, that they learn to will what was, in fact, the case—what they couldn't escape anyway. That is, in that story, death would follow, willynilly, such and such an act. Since that was the case, and couldn't be changed, they had two possible types of freedom open to them: either to assert their autonomy, live in illusion, and find out in the end that it was no autonomy; or to assent to the way things, alas, were, and see if the matter of freedom weren't something vastly different from what they might have supposed it to be. It was, according to that story, the way things are that the being called man exists as creature; the most noble creature, to be sure, but still creature; the lord of creation, yes, but holding that creation in vassalage to the great Lord of it all. That was the picture of human existence in the story, so that the question of freedom was one of discovering the conditions of that lordship and vassalage and assenting to them, rather than an idea of self-determination. The joker was, however, that they tried the latter idea. Like Pandora and the rest of us, they were convinced that it was worth doing what they inclined at the moment to do, and the devil take the consequences. Which is precisely what he did.

Freedom in that story, then, was a matter of uncoerced assent to what was given. Man, unlike the animals, was unique in his liberty to choose whether or not to offer that assent. But there was a scale of values in which freedom itself was not the *summum bonum*; it was ancillary to the greater matter of perfection. That is, *mere* self-determination would have been seen as tragically limiting, in that it cut one off from the Dance. Your freedom in the Dance is to be able to execute your steps with power and grace, not to decide what you feel like doing. The point, to that mind, was there *is*, like it or no, a Dance going on, and one may join or not. (One thinks of the Mock Turtle's "Will you, won't you, will you, won't you, won't you join the dance?") That option is a small freedom, to be sure; one isn't obliged to dance. But that option is not what is understood by the old myth as freedom.

Freedom would have been understood as something like power or joy. And it stood at the far end, often, of renunciation or denial or austerity. The implication, for instance, of the Adam and Eve story is that if they *had* bowed to the interdict placed on the forbidden fruit, life and not death would have been the guerdon. That is, paradoxically, if they had knuckled under to what looked emphatically like a *denial* of their freedom ("Thou shalt not" is not a very convincing corollary to the "Have dominion" charge), they would have discovered something unimaginable to them—something that, according to the story, was at that very point lost to them and us for the duration of human time.

The thing at stake in that story is at stake everywhere. What is the glory of the sun and moon and stars? Is it not at least partly that they exhibit a solemn and mathematical precision in their courses, a great astronomical sarabande or minuet? One doesn't think of the frug or the panic when one thinks of the stars. Whatever their glory is (and it registers itself on our consciousness as wholly satisfying, mathematically and aesthetically), it does not involve either self-determination or randomness. Similarly, what is the freedom of the athlete? His excellence is a matter of power—the power to *do* the thing beautifully. The perfection of the jump stands at the far end of a program of renunciation, in which his inclinations were subordinated to the demands of that very perfection. Or the race horse: there is something lovely about a wild horse snorting over the hill, but all that spirit and muscle must be brought under the rigor of bits and bridles and schedules *if* the special excellence of racing is sought. And the sonnet: here words dance in their highest dignity and beauty; here is language at its most excellent—but it is language dragooned and hedged and crowded and thwarted by *rules*. But, ironically, at the far end of those awful rules there emerges perfection. Or music: I may flog the keyboard with great zest for as long as I please, and a certain effect will be gained, and I may experience the release of whatever it is that wants to be thus released; but there is not a moment's comparison between that "freedom" and the austere perfection of a Mozart sonata. In the latter the notes are subordinated to a special design involving sequence and interval and rhythm and melody and harmony, and in that very subordination emerge in their own special excellence.

The old myth would have seen all these phenomena as images—images of some paradox that lay at the heart of things: that freedom for a thing is that state in which it appears at its highest performance (its perfection, in other words), and that this is a state that lies on the farther side of rigor and austerity. And it would have seen all these images as suggesting not a moral servility for that unique creature man, but rather the brilliant display, under a thousand forms, of the Dance, which goes on aeon after aeon, and which waits all breathless with hope for the Man to recognize the pattern, see his place, assent to it, and join. He may or he may not; that is his option. But his freedom is the ecstatic experience of the joyous measure whose music rings from galaxy to galaxy.

Chapter Seven

Sex

Under the new myth there has occurred what is being called a sexual revolution, in which brittle and frightened ideas which plagued other generations are being examined and discarded. The idea that energizes this reexamination is that sexuality is a normal and natural function of healthy people, that it contributes to the richness of human experience, and that adults can very well make up their own minds as to how they will understand and use this component in their makeup. There is a deep suspicion of the taboos with which other generations surrounded the phenomenon.

The viewpoint that is being described in this book has nothing to do with Victorianism, if by that we mean a frightened or reluctant view toward sexuality. Indeed, it would probably have to be located at the other end of the spectrum from that, in that it understands sexuality to be perhaps the supreme image in human experience of the way things are. It is at once an ebullient and an austere view.

This view would understand the division of man into male and female as, of course, a biological actuality; i.e., this is the way it *is*. It seems to be a necessity; it is at least a convenience; and it is certainly a delight. In any case, proceeding on the suspicion that the way things appear in our experience may be an image of the way they in fact are, and that to confront it all courageously might be to be nudged toward an awareness of a pattern, this view would inquire not only into the biological function of sexuality but also into the way in which the phenomenon has been handled by the human imagination, and further, into what the phenomenon yields when seen in various lights (e.g., as pure function; as the best overnight pleasure going; as the prize for strong attraction; as sacrament).

The human imagination seems always to have handled the phenomenon as a thing of enormous import. It is exceedingly difficult to find a tribe anywhere, or an era ever, that has had no consciousness of sexuality as being a hot potato, as it were. Anthropologists have never found the tribe to whom it makes no difference at all what man spends the night with what woman, and to whom the idea of *my* wives and *his* wives, or at least my concubines and his, has no content whatever; where sexuality exists on a par with breathing and defecating—one of the random functions of the human body, without the complicating ideas of intimacy and warrant with which the rest of humanity has set it about. And there are always the intensely appealing myths that tell us of arcadian groves where the god came down and lay at will with whatever nymph or shepherd boy took his fancy, and where the shepherds themselves could take their pleasure of whatever maiden came through the grove. But even in these old tales, there was always some vexing actuality that qualified the call to bliss: they at least had to get into a bower away from the public eye; and then the maiden might conceive, in which case there was a whole entail of difficulty; and, worst of all, they might find themselves having displeased some god or lover by their act, in which case there was no telling what furies they had let loose on the world.

The sense of humanity, in other words, has been that this blissful and procreative function is wildly charged with significance that reaches in all directions from the mere bed in which the two bodies happen to lie. We live in an epoch whose doctrine is that humanity may have been sadly mistaken and that the edge of the bed *is* as far as one can carry the significance. But this is a doctrine hardly borne out by the emotional experience of armies of outraged cuckolds and jilted lovers down through the centuries. In any case, we shall have to have scriptures weightier than *Playboy* to bring about the apocalyptic shift in sensibility that this idea asks. For it asks, in effect, that we scotch the whole corpus of poetry, myth, ritual, and drama by which the human imagination has, from the beginning of history, spoken of its apprehension of experience. I know of no serious work of the human imagination which proceeds upon the idea that there is nothing but dalliance in sexuality. Homer's immortality rests upon his high treatment of the phenomenon: the greatest heroes in the Western imagination concerned themselves with the question as to whose woman Helen might be. Where would Oedipus' difficulty be if plumbing were the only thing to be worried about in sex? Half the troubles that wracked the ancient world would not have occurred if the gods on Olympus had stayed out of each other's furtive liaisons instead of becoming jealous and taking the whole thing out on poor mortals below. Dante imagined sexuality as an energy that drove a man either toward perdition (Paolo and Francesca) or toward the Beatific Vision (his own immaculate experience of Beatrice). Chaucer showed two knights driven to distraction, despair,

courage, dissimulation, and combat by their attraction
to a single woman. Shakespeare had his Hamlet in an
agony over a question of sexual appropriateness, even
to the point of doubting the validity of his own life
and of human existence itself, and his Othello driven
mad by a jealousy that would be possible only in a
world in which the matter of sexuality was significant
infinitely beyond any question of brief pleasure or of
biology. Milton has sexuality take on a new and peculiar hue as a direct corollary to the disjuncture that occurred upon "man's first disobedience". And so on,
up through the novels of the eighteenth, nineteenth,
and twentieth centuries, and in the cinema which has
supplanted the novel as the major form to which the
human imagination has turned for a mode of utterance—sexuality is acknowledged as an energy that far
exceeds the biological and hedonistic description of it.
Which is to say that, in this realm of experience as in
the others we have looked at, the human imagination
transfigures what is, on one level, merely functional
into an occasion of significance. Whether it does this
by imposing some form upon the content, or by elic-
iting that form from the content, is never clear; for, as
in the case of painting, when the one thing has been
done ("imposing" the demands of color and mass and
line, etc., upon the Virgin and Child), it suddenly
seems as though the opposite were the case—as
though the form has arisen from the nature of the
subject.

But, it will be objected here, you have chosen your
works of imagination cleverly indeed, to support your
case. It's all very well to rake up Chaucer's Knight's
Tale, but what about all the rest of Chaucer? What

about his bawdy? What about the Miller's Tale or the
Summoner's Tale? What is Chaucer *really* known for?
And what about the great post-Enlightenment liberation of the human imagination from the solemnity of
the Dantes and Miltons? (Besides, these people all be-
longed to one religious viewpoint, and so you are beg-
ging the whole question. It is like a Buddhist trying to
urge a Buddhist point, and fetching up an array of
Buddhist authors to support him; naturally they will
say what he wants them to say.) I will have to concede
this point (except that I should think Homer and
Sophocles hardly fit), and admit that the Western
imagination of which I am speaking was by and large
determined by Christian categories, and that the question before the world now is whether those categories
are not, in fact, archaic and useless. But if the objection here is that it *was* all wrong, and that the race
labored under a pointless bondage for centuries, and
that the fields of joy ahead in which we will frolic free
of our fears about abstinence and continence and scru-
ple in sexuality promise more than was ever imaginable under the cold breath of superstition—if this is
your case, then *bon courage*: you have the brave task of
showing not only how the conflicts experienced by
the human imagination, from the mythic heroes on
down, were trivial, but also of indicating that your
new myth has deep roots in human experience and
that it will yield a richness of sensibility equaling that
which emerged from those old conflicts.

But what about bawdy then? What about Chaucer
and Shakespeare in their more robust moments, to
say nothing of Restoration drama and *Fanny Hill* and
Don Juan and Swinburne and then most of twentieth-

century literature? Is this not the record of the liberation struggle of the Western imagination from its thralldom to superstition? Are we not learning first to laugh at our own strictures, and then to cast them away? Is not the anal frankness of Chaucer the firstfruit of the twentieth-century candor that gives us Allen Ginsberg and Norman Mailer (both of them first-rate writers)? Aren't we getting closer to the freedom we want in direct ratio to the frequency with which we can utter scatological terms? Come. Let's not be so timorous about calling a spade a grub hoe.

There is this to be said of bawdy. When it occurs in serious literature, it occurs as a foil; that is, it appears in conscious and grinning contrast to whatever the serious theme may be. There is no such thing as an age that is not conscious of bawdy *as* bawdy—to whose imagination the word "fart", say (or some other, depending on the century), exists in exactly the same category as "hiccough". But let's face it—you cannot point out a *functional* hierarchy for the two bodily spasms of air. The facial expression that accompanies bawdy, if it is not a leer, is a twinkle. The characters in Chaucer who are famous for their bawdy (the Wife of Bath, the Miller, the Summoner) exist alongside the Knight and the Prioress and the Parson, whose tone is different. Ah, but we applaud precisely the courageous and good-humored realism that enabled Chaucer to accept and paint *both* these types. Yes, we do. But, in the first place, we must accept Chaucer's portrait of himself as a bit of a pixy; and in the second place, we must remember that the bawdy exists precisely *as* bawdy; that it is possible only in a context whose categories array things in such a way that seriousness is distinguishable from elvishness, and loftiness from vulgarity. The attempt in the twentieth century is, of course, to find a kind of freedom in which vulgarity will not be a category, since nothing "natural" (the usual things) will be disallowed. It is only the person who thinks that *appropriateness* is something to be pondered who looks upon the random and loud discussion of scatology and so on as perhaps vulgar. To the truly contemporary man who is out from under all the neurotic frigidity that recoiled from toilets and bedsheets, this is all anything but vulgar: it is honest and realistic and spontaneous and healthy, the idea being that vulgarity (of which bawdy is a light mode) exists only where there is some hierarchy of human action, with praying at the top and defecating at the bottom—and no such hierarchy exists, says the contemporary mind. And this book would say *d'accord*. No such simple hierarchy as *that* exists. There are no natural or necessary human functions that are regrettable, tawdry or in themselves sordid. (The view that says there are issues from the gnostic view of life which saw good and evil as in some way corresponding to spirit and flesh; it is a view which this book, along with Chaucer and Norman Mailer, would disavow.) If there is a hierarchy, it appears in terms of appropriateness, that is, that it is worth disposing human experience formally (as we do when we set the table for lunch, or shake hands, or write a sonnet)—that things do not appear in their own validity unless they are *set* right. The diamond is most excellently itself when it is cut; the edelweiss is most gloriously itself when it is not cut. The mountain is seen to best advantage from *here*; the music is best heard if that rattling fan is shut off, even though

we would like to have the fan going to keep us cool—
very well, then, we will have to make a choice as to
what we want, music or comfort. The idea is that
with respect to any phenomenon it is worth inquiring
into the terms in which it is most fully to be apprehended. There may be room for shuffling about: put
the rose *there* in the bouquet; no, there; no, try it by
itself, etc. Similarly, the human imagination has tried
its own experience, and the record of the quality that
emerges from the various disposings of that experience is there for us to look into: we shall have to decide if it is silly to see Dante's bouquet as setting off
the rose to more advantage than Ginsberg's.

So that the category "vulgar" does not imply some
gnostic arrangement of experience into high (spiritual
or intellectual) and low (digestive or procreative). It
implies, rather, a sense of appropriateness in which it
is no more seen as fitting to bring your digestive functions to the table than it would be to point out the
lurid birthmark on the face of the valedictorian. Both
topics are vulgar in that both are inappropriate *at that
point*. In the one instance, it does not mean that we
disallow digestion; indeed, an interesting case might
be made out in which the jolt involved in talking
about defecating during the lobster thermidor would
be traceable to a too radical juxtaposition of things—
that the transformation of the thermidor into waste
matter is not a process that can be contemplated with
equanimity while the thermidor is still thermidor, and
that therefore what we know superficially as decorum
or courtesy is simply the way the human imagination
has of coming to easy terms with the actualities of
experience. By the same token, no one holds the birth-

mark against the valedictorian; it is simply over-whelmingly irrelevant at this particular moment of recognition, and therefore grotesque, to point it out (and the vulgar may be a subdivision of the gro-tesque). *It* is not the grotesque thing now; *the pointing it out* is the great grotesquery. The outraged audience would not spend its time afterward gasping over the ugly valedictorian; its imprecations would be directed to the churl who took the occasion to point out that ugliness.

So that, with respect to bawdy, it is to be asked how it appears. If it appears as ancillary to the creation of a character who is himself a genuinely interesting char-acter (Sir John Falstaff, the Wife of Bath, etc.—and in-terestingness is itself a by-product of an awareness of the range of human possibilities either embodied in or aroused by that character)—if it appears thus, it may well be appropriate in its inappropriateness. If it throws other issues into relief, it may be well taken. If it is nothing at all but bawdy, it still may be saved by its tone, that is, by a certain levity that is fully aware of itself as precisely bawdy and nothing more. If it loses that twinkle and becomes a leer, then it has failed and is as worthless as pornography.

The human imagination, then, invests the sexual phenomenon with an importance that cannot be de-rived from any analysis of what seems to be occurring at the moment. Why, that is, should *this* kind of junc-ture of two bodies be so much more serious than *this* kind—say, shaking hands? Heretofore, of course, the shrill objection that children might issue from the one and not the other was a substantial one. But now, what with the pill and one thing and another, the objection has evaporated. Indeed, we are told that the pill throws the whole of traditional morality into a cocked hat, as though the possibility of children had been the *only* hedge about the act.

But the view I am speaking of here—the view which suspects that the way the serious human imagination has handled the phenomenon may not be far from the truth of the matter—this view would understand the division of man into male and female as suggesting something worth considering. That is, whatever might be suggested to us by the phenomenon of man, we experience that phenomenon under two modes, male and female. The one mode has seemed to embody some such qualities as strength and courage and sovereignty, and the other gentleness and nourishment and care. And in the male and female *images*, these qualities have seemed to inhere in the hard, sinewy, hairy litheness of the one body, and in the soft, breasted fairness of the other. There appeared to be a correspondence between the *form* of the image and the nature of the being. To be sure, there were Amazons and Valkyries and so on, but they were prodigies and not typical. The Amazon, that is, was not archetypal woman; she was woman-as-warrior. The image of the male suggested the fountainhead of life with its sources springing from strength; the image of the female suggested the fecund matrix in which that life took nourishment and form. Here myth and biology were indistinguishable.

And more. Oddly, the rite of life, this most common and most mysterious thing, describable both by plumbing and mystic terms, appearing as both ridiculous and noble, slimy and sublime—this was not only the rite of life, but of knowledge. That is, the act which generated life was at the same time the act which signaled the high point of knowledge between two beings. It suggested that the nature of that knowledge between the one mode and the other was fruitful. The old term was "know". Adam *knew* his wife. But it was a form of knowledge that asked a warrant. It stood both at the end and at the beginning: at the end not only of a pursuit but of a committal—I will be yours if you will be mine; and at the beginning—of a peculiarly exclusive relationship. Zeus had a wife, no matter what nymphs he might visit, and he knew Hera was his wife, and she knew Zeus was supposed to be her husband, and from that idea there arose the quarrels whose olympian fallout so often blighted things below. Solomon had three hundred wives and seven hundred concubines, but there was no mistake about whose they were; they were the King's, and let the rest of you jolly well keep your hands off. Even here there was a committal: the King took it upon himself to provide for his harem. (This book, incidentally, presents no argument for monogamy. I do not think it can be proved to have some exclusive and ultimate legitimacy, although I do suspect that it might be the *best* arena in which the great and binding experiment can be carried out. The record of polygamy, even in the case of our father Abraham, seems often to be a record of difficulty.) The committal that preceded the sexual union was that you both give yourself to me and take me, and I do likewise vis-à-vis you. This agreement is then enacted bodily: the act is successful only to the extent that you both give yourself to me and take me and I do likewise vis-à-vis you. Otherwise, it turns into nightmare and rape.

But it was understood most emphatically as an enactment in whose rites there is seen played out in bodily form exactly what cries out to be expressed thus. That is, the desire in a man to *know* that woman —the desire that is aroused by her appearance and her voice and her mien—wants to find some form under which it can shape itself; the form, in other words, that will deliver it from rushing about ghostlike in the ether of his imagination. The form may at first be distant: the attentiveness of small courtesies. Then it may exist verbally: in conversation, itself proceeding from general chitchat toward greater and greater intensity and intimacy. Then, finally, it finds its perfect form in the enactment by the two unveiled images, the images of male and female, of the energy that strains toward total union. That is, the thing that I want passionately to know, while I am aware that it appears only under this fleshly image and is itself more than that image, I can know only via the greatest possible experience of that image.

Here the distinction between spirit and matter disappears, as it does in the Sacraments. For here I experience the oddity that flesh is the mode under which I apprehend the truth of the thing. It is the epiphany of the thing. There is, in the sexual rite, a sense of struggle. It is the mad straining of the two images to get through to the very center of the thing (and this is not merely a pun; according to the view being put here, the anatomical placing of things would be itself a perfect image of what is at work in the situation, so that the fact that the final rite occurs at the "center" of the bodies is to be expected). There is, ironically, in this most soaring of all satisfactions a radical sense of incompleteness. The ecstasy accompanies the *exploration*, an exploration that never quite finds that ultimate elysium where the union is unimaginable to us, but toward which union we strain again and again, and which very attempt we find to be ecstatic.

There is at work in the rite the awareness of *the other*. The nature of any union is such that it follows only upon the junction of separate things. You can't have a union of one thing. That is a solitude. A union requires at least two elements. There is a distinct kind of satisfaction that attends union: in chemistry you bring two things together in the compound that you want—say, water; in music you bring two notes together and get harmony; in human affairs you bring people together and form a community that makes possible a certain *esprit* and solidarity not possible to one man alone. In the sexual realm the union involved is that of the two modes under which man appears, male and female. It is the effort by both to know the *other*, but *the other which is also itself.* This may be the point at which the human imagination has traditionally suspected masturbation, homosexuality, incest, bestiality, etc., to be less than the desideratum.

Masturbation would represent a form of solipsism, that is, the attempt to seize the special kind of pleasure (orgasm) that attends the carnal knowledge of the other when the other is present only in fantasy; hence it would represent also a denial of the idea that authentic meaning emerges only from the real union of form (the ritual act between two bodies) and content (the quest for knowledge of the other). That is, the individual masturbating is seeking one of the benefits of union with the other while at the same time in effect disavowing the importance of that other by acting in solitude. Even in this forlorn act there would be, perhaps, levels of pathos, with the person who at least tries to summon the other in fantasy not sunk quite so far into Gomorrah as the person who is aroused and gratified only by the image of his own body.

Similarly, homosexuality would be a case in point of recoil from the other. It seeks the ecstatic union with a second image, to be sure, but with an image that is not an image of the other mode under which man appears, the opposite sex. It fears to go out of itself in quest and exploration of the other, to give itself to the other in conquest and surrender, and to receive the same from the other. It seeks this exchange with an image that is a repeat of itself, and there is no analogy in all heaven and earth for such a thing—for significance (or fruit, or meaning) following upon the union of identicals. On all levels, there is this union of differences: of positive and negative charge, of stamen and pistil, of cock and hen, of god and goddess. At the very origin of man himself, the god (masculine) comes to the earth (feminine), and into the image which he forms from the stuff of her body he breathes the breath of life. And in the supreme instance of all, when it is time for him to appear among men, the Incarnate does not issue straight from the godhead but rather from the fecund visitation of the Holy Ghost upon the body of the Virgin Lady.

It may be objected that fruit is not the object of a homosexual relationship; it is, at its best, an expression of love. The only rejoinder to this would be the whole argument of this book—the idea that things are not random; that one thing signals another; that there is an antiphon sounding among all things in the universe; that what appears *here* may throw light on that over *there*; indeed, that it is probably a case in point of the same thing. If this has any validity (and one must always stop short of inquisition in pressing an argument like this), the kind of union sought under homosexual conditions would be no union at all, but only the parody of a union, since the suggestion of all things from physics to biology to myth bespeaks a pattern in which authentic union involves *different modalities of the same thing*: "different", as in electrons and protons, or male and female, so that it is union and not mere juxtaposition (you can't fuse two electrons); "of the same thing", so that we don't find sweet peas and sea gulls cohabiting, or turtles and gazelles.

Again, incest is like homosexuality in that it does not find an image appropriately differentiated from itself. It is of the same blood, and it is not only on the biological level that we see monstrosity issuing from the union: the roles of mother and wife do not mix. Insofar as they are enacted by one person, they are enacted with respect to different partners. A boy may not approach his mother with the sexual rite in mind any more than a husband may try to make his wife over into a mother figure. Both attempts are confusion. Appropriateness is the test, and no merely scientific analysis of the situation will tell us why *this* body may not cohabit with this one. The forms are there (male body, female body), but the roles do not permit it. Again, to argue that it is only prudery that has thrown up these roadblocks in the way of appetite (presumably some people *do* want their mothers or their sisters) is to argue that the whole of human sensibility is awry.

Bestiality would likewise be a failure to discern the other rightly, for in this case, the other would be too radically other, and no union would be imaginable. That is, the physical rite would signal nothing at all but orgasm, and where there is form (male and female in cohabitation) without content (the rite as sign of real union), there is chaos. No such union between a man and a dog is thinkable. There may be affection between a man and his dog, and trust, and companionship, and a kind of joy. The dog may lick the man's face and even sleep with him. But carnal activity between the two images would be like the effort to appreciate a sonata with your nose; it would be bringing the wrong capacity to bear on the situation. There is nothing in dogdom which is to be apprehended by humankind via sexuality, although there is a great deal in dogdom which brings intense pleasure to us. But here as in the other cases, the scientific and hedonistic approaches to the question will discover nothing on the face of the green earth to show why a man should not love his dog to the point of carnality. It is only on the mythic and imaginative level that valuation is possible.

Promiscuity, either homosexual or heterosexual, is another form of failure to discern the other authentically, for it focuses on the body not as image but as object alone. The sailor who desperately needs something during his overnight in port, the junior executive with his list of telephone numbers in the convention city, the college boy cruising the beach, the old queen in the bar—none of these people feels malicious or even evil. Each has an appetite, there is a perfectly simple way to assuage that appetite, so *en avant*. But the ritual which they seek is a parody. It is like a Black Mass. For both involve all the equipment, movement, and pantomime of the real thing, and both promise a reward indistinguishable at the moment from the reward of the real thing (orgasm; supernatural food). But they are not addressed to the object which the ritual was designed to address. In the Mass, man addresses God and he addresses man, and there is a communion under the species of bread and wine; in sexual intercourse we address the other and the other addresses us, and there is a communion under the species of human anatomy. In the case of bread and wine, of course, it is possible and permissible to throw it away from a picnic table; but the minute you have set it about with a particular intention and ritual it is transformed, and you may no longer throw it away. By the same token, the human body is available for any number of activities (sports, medical inspection, work), but when it is taken into the service of the sexual rite, a universe of significance comes upon it, like God into the Mass, and immediately the participants are less than the thing in which they are participating, and it is theirs to observe the rubric with awe. The equipment is no longer merely object; it is image. Taken into the rite, it is transformed. As in poetry, courtesy, ceremony, or any of the ritual ways in which we shape our experience, so here the imposing of a form upon mere function paradoxically elicits the true significance of that function from the raw material. So, for the sailor, the businessman, the boy, and the old queen, another human body is by far the best means of getting a certain kind of pleasure. But it also happens that the human body is the epiphany of

personhood. It cloaks and reveals a human individual.
A doctor may probe it strictly as a complex of organs
and tissue; a gymnastics coach may manipulate it as a
pattern of muscles. But the sexual exploration of this
mass of tissue and muscle puts the bread and wine on
the altar: the real presence of the person must now be
reckoned with. The sailor sweating over the strum-
pet's body is like a priest rushing into the tabernacle
and gobbling the bread for a snack. The executive
with his call girl, the boy with his trick, the queen
with his hustler all participate in the Black Mass
which divides form and substance, for it takes the
form (the body) and discards the substance (the person); it takes the form (the rite of two bodies) and discards the substance (the union of two persons).

There is also dramatized in the sexual rite the human consciousness of privacy. We can see at work here
exactly the same thing that manifests itself in a thousand other ways in our experience—the mystery of
privacy, the exclusiveness of privacy, and the special
pleasure of finally being admitted into the private.

We are all familiar enough with the mystery that
attends the private. Half the excitement of the books
we read when we were young attached to what was *in*
the bound chest, or what was behind the sealed door,
or what awful story lay in the bundle of letters in the
locked drawer in the little room in the attic. What
secret knowledge did the old crone carry with her
behind those beady eyes? What did she have in the
satchel gripped in her gnarled claw under that black
cloak? What went on in that castle tower where the dim
blue light shone every night at midnight? We were

aroused, that is, by the very *fact* of something private and unavailable.

But sometimes the mystery suggested an ecstatic rather than a horrible revelation. The tall knight who appeared to us in the gusty wood and who lifted us to his saddle—where was he taking us? Not yet, little one; trust me. You shall see. There are many dangers ahead, but if you will be strong and brave and patient, you shall see. Wait. Or the beautiful and kindly lady with the shining face who beckoned us silently with a finger to her lips. She would not tell us her secret, but we knew it was worth waiting for. All these situations called to something in us that was intensely aware that secrecy, or privacy, is in the cards, and that it is a higher consciousness that bows to this and waits for the time and the permission, than that which shouts, "Open it now! I want it now! I shall have it at once!"

And not only does privacy suggest mystery to us, and hence the privilege of revelation, or admission; it also implies exclusiveness. We see this, too, in common experience. We have all passed great lawns hidden behind well-tailored shrubbery at whose only entrance we are rebuffed with Private Property: Keep Out. The public, sweltering in the bumper-to-bumper crawl along the highway to the beach, must all go to *that* beach, not this, since this one says Members Only—and what joy if we happen to be members. How many of us have perched and twisted on a wooden bench during a Channel crossing or at an airport, and gazed enviously at the closed door marked First Class Passengers Only. Or even inside the club itself, there is the special armchair ("That's where the big man himself always sits"). And of course we are familiar enough with the hallowed: only the initiated are allowed through this veil; only the sibyl may go in there; only the High Priest may enter the Holy of Holies.

The point in all this exclusion and debarring is that the very nature of the spot is lost the instant it is thrown open to all and sundry. The private beach is no better than Coney Island if the Keep Out sign is taken down. The quiet terrace overlooking the great park behind the château where the earl and countess used to sit with their friends in the cool of the evening—now that the château has been opened to the public, it is trodden by a thousand draggled couples with crying infants, and evening only brings the park attendants with burlap bags to pick up the Kleenex and popsicle papers. The Holy of Holies is desecrated, now that the invading soldiers have rushed in, torn down the veil, drunk the wine, and melted the altar of gold. It existed only so long as it was cut off from the public.

The human imagination has supposed that there is something not only desirable but inevitable about the setting apart of things. When they are thus set, they partake of that very setting apart, so that the bread *inside* the tabernacle, although it differs by not a single molecule from this bread out here in the old woman's basket, may not be sold in the marketplace. In the case of the holy, that is, a sense of desecration follows upon the random opening up of what was hidden or set apart. In the case of the secular (the beach, the château), desecration is a word that, although it is certainly used by those who hate to see the stampede, is perhaps too strong. But whatever it is that occurs when we open up what has been reserved or set apart or fenced off for special and privileged use, something unmistakable has disappeared and it is not the same now.

It may be objected here that this line of thought leads to the obnoxious idea that such and such a grove of trees *ought* only to be enjoyed by the privileged few—that, by some incredible aristocratic notion, the few are the only ones qualified to appreciate these trees; or, conversely, that these trees are such that they are not to be appreciated by any but the few. This is not the argument. The idea is simply that, for whatever reasons, there is a unique quality that attaches to the thing that has, in fact, been set apart, that is private or holy, and that the destruction of the special apartness entails the disappearance of that particular quality.

This, of course, raises the question as to whether such and such an instance of the private *ought* perhaps, in the interest of the good, to be broken into. And this can be answered only by inquiring into the nature of what is housed in the barred area. If it is the President's office, we feel that it is right that privacy be preserved, since most of what is discussed there is of such a nature that its public airing would issue only in uproar. On the other hand, if the private place is a torture chamber or a grotto where the bomb plots are hatched, we all feel that the privacy had better be invaded. In the eighteenth century, the citizens of France felt that the royal privileges were perpetuating monstrous injustices, and so everything was all torn down. Two views are possible here: either that *this particular situation* demanded such a tearing down since it had gone rotten, or that *any* situation of exclusiveness and privilege must be torn down—in which case the revolutionaries themselves would have had to disband their secret councils and their own governing hierarchies. George Orwell's *Animal Farm* is a brilliant parable, for besides illustrating the cynicism that throws down one set of privileges only to set up another, it suggests the inevitability of privilege in any human affairs. The pigs, who complain that the farmer is enjoying unfair privileges, lead the animals in a revolt and drive the farmer away from the farm. Within a few weeks, however, the pigs are lounging in the farmhouse, directing the work of the commune, and the horse is working himself literally to death at the farm drudgery. Whether it is the glittering court of Louis or Nicholas, or the White House, or the Kremlin, or the tent in which Fidel sits, there is always a fenced-off area.

The human imagination has treated the sexual phenomenon as a fenced-off area. Let us have no cant about Victorian prudery's creating the rigid conditions that surround it. In all cultures, in all epochs, there has been this sense of privacy, of exclusion, of privilege, marking it off. Different cultures manifest this awareness differently, of course. I know two women, each of whom lived with what we would call a primitive tribe—the one with the Nuers in East Africa, the other with the Aucas in Ecuador. Neither tribe wore so much as G strings. Both tribes practiced polygamy. Obviously, then, they had a slightly different sensibility than ours regarding sexual matters. They certainly were not Victorian or Puritan. They were the modern man's dream tribe—naked, free, unembarrassed. But they were not his dream. For both tribes had laws about sexuality as austere as the laws of the Medes and the Persians. The Nuers had vivid public puberty rites, but the rites did not in the least suggest a lack of awareness that sexual union was something strictly set apart for only those with the warrant. In neither tribe was there any confusion at all as to the warrant for sexual intercourse. Fornication was as furtive and dangerous as it was in Massachusetts Bay Colony.

But the vastly different ways that Danes and aborigines and Mandarins and Sioux and Greeks have had of handling the phenomenon have this in common, that they *set it apart*. The mystery and rigor that surround it do not derive only from the biology of the thing, although there is a great deal to be said for the idea that the awareness of fruitfulness is what arouses the ceremony that surrounds sexuality, so that primitive tribes have sexual rituals corresponding to their vegetation rituals, the common denominator being fruitfulness. But this does not explain why men, as opposed to birds, isolate and hallow what is important to them. Seedtime and harvest are important to the life of the tribe, and so we find spring and autumn rituals, involving the formal and ceremonious enacting of what is being marked.

Sexuality, then, is a fenced-off area. We must ask whether, like the Holy of Holies, the veil ought to be torn down, or whether it does, in fact, house the god. Will the breaking down be desecration or emancipation?

The modern answer is that it is emancipation. The answer comes to us in a thousand forms. It comes in the serious statements of anthropologists, psychologists, and theologians, that the race has been all wrong and that we are in a new world where "man come of age" may accept his inclinations as guidelines to conduct. It comes in the pronouncements of journals such as *Playboy* and *The East Village Other* that continence and abstinence and fidelity are really rather quaint. It comes, of course, in pornography, where the assumption is that the excitement of the moment is the only test, so that this body is worth more than that one because the legs are more appealing, etc. But it comes to us, perhaps most effectively, in the unexamined assumptions underlying nearly all of current fiction, cinema, drama, and journalism, that the ticket into the fenced-off area is simply desire.

The view which is being put in this book, however, is that the rush into the fenced-off place is a desecration and not an emancipation. It proceeds upon the assumption first that the idea of the private, the set apart, is a legitimate one, and that on the one hand it is not only worthwhile but necessary that some things be set apart, and that on the other, there are some things whose very nature demands such a setting apart (diamonds, for instance, or the taste of fresh raspberries, or letters from one's lover). Second, it would suspect that the human imagination has not been mistaken in handling the sexual phenomenon as one of the things to be set apart in the exclusive place.

It would suspect this because it would see the body as the image of the person, and the person as a thing vast and mysterious and not to be raided. Who *am* I? Oh, to be sure, I have such and such a job, and live in such and such a city, and studied at this university and that, and grew up in that town, and am so and so's brother, and am married to so and so. But this is all cocktail party stuff. It is true enough, but incidental. It is not *who* I am. Who am I? God only knows. My mother knows me to a certain extent; and my brothers and sisters do; and my friends; and each of these after the mode appropriate to that relationship. But insofar as I exist as a son to someone, the mode of knowledge appropriate in that relationship is filial, with all that that entails of obedience and honor and trust and affection, and not sexual. Likewise, insofar as I exist as a brother to someone, the mode of knowledge which that person has of me is fraternal and not sexual. Also with my friends: a few know me in ways that no family member does, but again, their knowledge of me does not come to them under the sexual modality.

Where, then, is the sexual mode of knowledge appropriate? It is in that sanctum known to the whole race of men as marriage. Never mind what sort of rite marks the public occasion (church ceremony, justice of the peace, seven-day fiesta, Abraham going into the tent to Sarah, Solomon taking another woman for his wife, or a Nuer purchasing a girl from her father for so many cattle). The human imagination has set the sexual rite into this veiled sanctum. It does not occur in the marketplace, or at the table, or in the drawing room. Not even the parody of it (whoredom) occurs there. One goes behind closed doors. But the closed wooden doors are themselves only the sign of the closed doors behind which the human imagination keeps the phenomenon. They are not the closed doors of embarrassment, or of shame, although some eras have acted as though they were. Rather, they are like

the veil into the holy place: up to *here* you may all
come, but I must go alone beyond here, in unto this
personhood whose being is to be opened under this
particular modality to me alone. (And of course the
physical actualities of the rite so exactly correspond to
this awareness of entry into the secret place beyond
the veil that they hardly need pointing out.)

Of course, there is a great deal of huggermugger
traffic. This is a possibility in any sanctum. There is
always some mercenary priestess who will give you a
peep for a small fee. There is always some voyeur who
will keep opening the secret door for a look at the
mysterious stone. And of course, all of us incline to
feel at one point or another that the warrant for an
entrance into the holy place is simply desire, and not
the anointing to the priesthood of this altar. And there
is no denying it: the reward is apparently there for
whoever wants to go in and take it. No dragon seems
to guard the shrine. No bolt of divine fury blasts the
interloper. All may come and go at will.

So it seems. But those who honor the shrine begin
to participate in an exchange and a communion whose
nature eludes those who traffic in the holy things. The
traffickers always seem to have the advantage: we are
getting more and better and greater variety than you:
How can you argue that your monotonous, repeti-
tious, exclusive little ritual is more exciting and rewarding than this delectable variety? Well, it is a bit
hard to make it make sense, and by *your* tests, of
course (variety, delectability), it doesn't compare.

But, oddly, those who honor the shrine move, by
their very attendance on the rubric, toward some
great and unimagined Unveiling when the ecstatic se-

cret is opened to those who have learned that no churl will see the Holy Thing; to those who have learned that it is not by pushing into a thousand shrines that one becomes able to pass through that final Veil, but rather by brave and single attendance on the one shrine committed to one; who know that an unveiling is a real unveiling only to the extent that what is veiled is set apart from the other things around, and that one's appreciation of the reward is in some ratio to what one has experienced of patience in waiting for it; and to those who have received the ecstatic communion entrusted to them as an image of some final Communion when the knowledge of all beings will be ecstatic; who, by their participation in the rite (or by their wait for it—those who for one reason or another are denied the foretaste here) have apprehended the knowledge of other beings as a high and holy thing, not to be flung open at random.

Chapter Eight

Bravo the Humdrum

But it is not all a matter of metaphysics and aesthetics and ethics. Or, if it is (and in a sense, everything that concerns any human being comes to that sooner or later), it doesn't present itself to our consciousness that way. We can't spend every day contemplating the cosmos; we have neither the time nor the stamina. It would be like living on chateaubriand and fine old burgundy three times a day. There would come a time (probably after the second meal) when one would hanker for a boiled potato and a glass of milk. That is, whatever may lie behind things, one still has to live one's life, and it doesn't much matter whether or not the baby is a case in point (an image) of something eternal; he is still shrieking unhappily and needs to be *changed*. And the diapers are just as objectionable, no matter whether the process means everything or nothing. Living one's life ordinarily means up at seven or eight, dishes, laundry, baby, vacuuming, shopping, and cooking (if one is a housewife), or rush hour, desk, lunch, desk, rush hour (if one is a professional person).

But if all this sort of thing has anything to do with what life might really be *about*, it ordinarily escapes us. These seem to be the things that one must get through in order to get at what it's really about.

This is a notion that operates in all of us, and there is a public imagery that has developed in our epoch (as any epoch develops its imagery) that appeals to this notion. The imagery varies, but the idea is the same. It is that the humdrum necessities of life are just that —humdrum—and that one begins to live when one shifts one's attention to other things.

The most arresting image of recent years is the hippie image and its derivatives. Here there is a disavowal of the competitiveness and mechanization and brutalization of the modern world, and an attempt to return to simplicity, spontaneity, and earthiness. To outsiders it looks like one more kind of conformity. (Who ever saw a hippie in a starched collar and herringbone suit? What hippie would have the courage to appear in that uniform?—his friends wouldn't *accept* it, any more than Chase Manhattan would accept his beads and sheepskins.) But to the people who accepted the ideas about human life which are displayed in the costume, it is a perfectly serious and acceptable pageant. One signals one's individuality or one's whim or one's preference by dressing as a Basque shepherd, or a cossack, or George Washington, General Pershing, or John the Baptist. Why be stamped out of Brooks Brothers' machines like so many English muffins on a conveyor? And one seeks an approach to (or an escape from) actuality in various forms of herb and chemical, exactly as one's old mother sought it in the Rosary or the PTA, or one's father in the martini or the club. These things are entirely determined by one's imagination as to what is important (or desirable) and how it looks. The old woman with the Rosary felt that it was important to take a certain amount of time to perform an act of devotion and intercession, since there was someone she had never seen behind everything she could see who was, in the end, more important than the laundry and the cooking. Even if her act deteriorated into the somnolence of mere habit (which it sometimes did), she would have been vigorously reawakened to what she had originally thought was important if you had suddenly told her that she could *not* say her Rosary anymore. This is not to say that she had ever really thought through the whole thing and was prepared to give you a convincing rationale for what she was doing, any more than the young hippie's rationale for his pot could stand much scrutiny. It is simply to say that we do what we think is important, or what will bring us a result that we want (answered prayer, less time in purgatory, two hours of euphoria, whatever).

In any case, the hippie imagery is one that has attracted the attention of everyone, the approval of many, and the solemn loyalty of thousands. But it is not the only imagery by which the modern world organizes its daily life. Another of the popular sets of imagery as to what life ought to look like is what might be called the *Esquire-Playboy–Town and Country* imagery. This looks at first like a rather mixed bag, but the idea celebrated in the imagery of these publications is one which understands youth, money, travel, beauty, taste, and connections to be of the essence. That is, just as the old *Saturday Evening Post* used to seem a sort of hebdomadal bible celebrating old-shoe domesticity, rural virtue, and plucky Americana (*vide* Norman Rockwell's covers), so these publications create and nourish an idea that appeals to a different imagination. Here the images are of gorgeous young men and women (French or Italian nobility, if possible) dressed, coiffed, and scented by Gucci, Pucci,

Cassini, Balenciaga, Valentino, Bill Blass, Hermes, Cardin, or Kenneth. In this world the thing to be sought is not so much the simplicity and earthiness of the hippie, or the gingham and piecrust of Norman Rockwell, as the afterdeck of somebody's cruiser in the Aegean. The idea energizing the imagery here is that the taxing and pedestrian demands of domesticity (laundry, chicken pox, the A&P, the 8:05) are either to be fled from altogether, or understood as a bore. That's what people in Endsville do all day long. *Life* begins at the travel agent's desk, or at the boutique counter, or with the coveted invitation. No one supposes that the whole world is populated with the gorgeous types who people the ads and pictorial specials of these journals, but everyone knows that there are enough people who will spend their lives either trying to gain a foothold in that world, or adoring it vicariously, to make the imagery profitable.

There is also what might be called the Procter and Gamble–*Good Housekeeping* imagery. This rises from the awareness that, Gucci and the Aegean notwithstanding, most people do, in fact, have to mop and dust and launder, and that these activities may as well be placed in as minimal and euphemistic a light as possible since they represent plebeian necessities that obstruct what a human being might otherwise be doing all day long. The imagery here is of crisp, svelte young wives gliding over mahogany tabletops with a magic spray, or rejoicing in fluffy dunes of snowy sheets just out of the machine.

These are disparate images with which the contemporary imagination is hailed, and they have, oddly enough, that common idea, that the humdrum is *here* and the real stuff over *there*—if not in the Haight-Ashbury pad, on the Aegean, and if not there, at the country club or book review circle while the wash-rinse cycle completes itself. There is a quest, that is, for interest and significance somewhere other than in the humdrum.

Now it will be suspected that I am about to urge some return to a neo-Vermeer kitchen with mother, all rosy and buxom, puffing over the washboard, and father, lovable old clout that he is, trudging along the furrow behind the oxen. Fie on travel; fie on clubs; fie on boutiques and *haute couture* and discothèques.

No. For one thing, there are no more washboards and oxen to speak of, and for another, if you can get it done with a Westinghouse or an International Harvester, so much the better.

It is a matter of values. That is, whatever has been gained for us by technological advance, if it has led us to believe that the humdrum is a prison, and that "life" lies beyond its small borders, there has been something wrong. There is an irony, of course, in the elusiveness of the very thing that all the technology claims to be *about*, namely, an increase of human freedom. The spirits of twentieth-century man are not notably more blithe and amiable than those of his seventeenth-century fathers. Simultaneous with our apparent release from the humdrum via technology, there has occurred an increase in vexation, frustration, and ennui in the human experience of life. And this vexation seeks some resolution in the imagery we have already noted, an imagery that represents release, liberty, variety, fascination.

It is not that there is something more virtuous or fulfilling about a woman's spending six hours at the hearth to prepare a meal rather than forty-five minutes in an electronic kitchen (although there might be in a world different from ours, who knows?). It is, rather, that it is possible, according to one viewpoint, to see necessity as the very occasion of glory; or, put another way, to see *the given* as both concealing and revealing something significant about the way things are.

It comes around, in other words, to a matter of the old myth and the new. Somehow the new, in the name of autonomy and freedom, has managed to place burdens on the human spirit too heavy to be borne. They seem to weigh us down more than the fears of goblins and hell weighed our fathers down. It may be the burden of knowledge. Or it may be the burden of freedom: What in heaven's name shall we *do* with ourselves? Whatever it is, it has produced a bloody century, a suicidal century, a disenchanted century, a century requiring the services of healers wholly unknown to our fathers, namely, psychiatrists.

It is an ironic perdition, in that, *in the name of the immediate*, we have lost our grip on the immediate. That is, in the name of the reality we could see and handle, we disavowed the gods who, our fathers thought, had stood behind things, and who, we thought, had kept us from becoming masters of our own world; but, by becoming sole masters of that world, we suddenly found out that we may have become masters of something worth no more than a clinker. We had thought that the way to appreciate and master things was to snip away the metaphysical skein that tangled those things up with the eternal, and to look at them as themselves and nothing more. So that to us a mountain is only that thrusting up of strata that you see there, impressive, to be sure—even beautiful—but not really to be thought of as a case in point (an image) of anything *eternal*; and blood is a vital fluid that we find circulating through our bodies, performing this and that function, and may be spoken of *poetically* (i.e., fancifully) as representing the life of life, but it is very unscientific to understand it as an image displaying under its own conditions something really serious about the way things are; and sexuality is both vital and fun, but it is itself and not a carnal figuration of relationships that lie at the very heart of everything.

The focus on things for their own sake has a very great deal to commend it, but somehow that focus made it easy (perhaps unavoidable) for the mass of unthinking modern men to believe that it really *was* a case, as Poe's poor hero found, of "only this and nothing more". It is nearly impossible for the convinced modern mind to understand how a thing can be looked at as an image and at the same time as a thing valid and glorious in itself. "Well, if it's only an image, it's only a dream, then. You've got some vaporous and idealistic philosophy that denies the reality of things. It's mysticism, and that is hardly palatable to the twentieth century."

No again. The viewpoint being described in this book would accept neither the positivism that insists that it is "only this and nothing more" nor the idealism that says that this isn't really it at all. It celebrates the hard reality and beauty of things in themselves—things that need no transcendent apologia (borzois, mountains, dolphins, sex, wine, babies), and sees this reality as appearing simultaneously and paradoxically as itself and as image. Not as mirage but as image. Not as allegory but as image. Not as illusion but as a case in point, under its own species, of the way things are.

This view would understand the sense of ennui and alienation that plagues our epoch to be the natural corollary to the disavowal of the eternal from which derives the validity of everything that appears in our experience. For it would say that, sooner or later, the human imagination, which is forever asking for significance, will find it frustrating to be told that it is not to *ask* the question of significance, since that is not a property of things. Well, if *this* doesn't mean anything then (the imagination replies), does *this*? No? Well, then, let's look over here. What about this? No? Well, here then. No again? Alas, the world is weary, stale, flat, and unprofitable. This is, of course, the burden of the twentieth-century chorus. It is in flat-out pursuit of something that will reassure, amuse, and stimulate it. The common stuff of life has nothing to be said for it except that it is necessary and boring, and hence one must seek what one's imagination wants in the new, the varied, the bizarre, the remote, and the intense. Hence the jet set, hence high fashion, hence pot and hallucinogens and random sex and happenings and the avant-garde syndrome.

What then? Shall we stop traveling? Is Bulgaria not interesting? What's the matter with chic clothes? Shall we take up knitting? Shall we slouch along exactly fifty years behind whatever is occurring at any point in history?

No again. Again it is a matter of values and sensibility. The thing itself (travel, sex, clothing, drugs, entertainment) is there, to be used one way or another by people. A man is no more culpable for traveling than he is for drinking a glass of wine. Both are good and pleasurable experiences. But the man who turns more and more to travel to fend off the fear of the humdrum is like the man who turns more and more to wine to fend off that fear: he had better take a look at his priorities and see what it is that he is afraid of. The woman who experiences her uxorial and maternal tasks as a prison, and who feels that she is alive only to the extent that she is "out and about"—that woman clearly has a set of priorities in which the roles of wife and mother are subordinate to other roles (hostess, chairwoman, golfer, courtesan, whatever). The unmarried career person who finds his (or her) attention more and more commandeered by the bars, parties, theaters, discothèques, and weekends that hold out some variation on the humdrum might inquire into the possibilities of seeing that very humdrum as the agent and mediator of something substantial.

For in the effort to escape *into* this or that *from* whatever we find in our laps, there is implied a discrepancy, a hiatus, between necessity and aspiration—between what we find life for us to be made up of, and what we wish it were made up of. This frustration is one of the corollaries of the new myth.

The old myth would have seen the given (the humdrum, in most cases) as, on the other hand, precisely the agent and mediator of something substantial—of the way things are, in a word. This is not to say that everyone up to the Enlightenment went whistling about the kitchen and the farmyard, merry and content in the knowledge that his broomstick or shovel was the *summum bonum*. It is simply to say that the old myth itself sanctioned the humdrum by seeing it, along with everything else in the world, as image. That is, the commonplaces of life, the given rhythms of experience in which every human being is involved whether he is king or serf, jet set or typist (things like birth, growth, learning, work, marriage, and friendship), are themselves the occasions in which we may enact what is real, what lies at the root of things. In this view, there is no hiatus between what we are given to do by life and what life is "really about". There is, on the contrary, a synonymity. All this commonplace stuff *is* what life is really about. Three cheers for travel and the theater and parties and fashions, but they aren't at the center. What is at the center is the given, the obvious—things like birth and growth and work and learning and marriage. For it is to these things that all drama and poetry and music stand at one remove; it is of these things that art itself speaks. One goes to the theater to see—what? To see the ritual reenactment of what, presumably, we in the audience have some point of contact with in our own experience. The drama may be a drawing-room farce, an orgy, a space fantasy, a gothic horror, but each of these enacts something that finds an antiphon in our own experience: familiar laughter, passion, the conflict of good and evil, terror, etc. What occurs on the far side of the footlights (or up and down the aisles, in this day of living theater) is at best one remove from the centers of human experience, precisely because it is contrived and hemmed in and deliberately organized to involve the audience (there are still *audience* and *actors*) in some mime. No one *really* gets shot; that would be living theater with a vengeance. The same is true of opera, which depends not so much on dramatic subtlety as on a musical figuration of the human experiences at work in the situation, so that in *Tosca*, for instance, you get in the arias a case in point, under the species of the human voice, of the agony that is being enacted, or of terror in *Faust*, or of innocence in *The Magic Flute*. It is more than just a song *about* agony or terror or innocence. Similarly, in "pure" music (concerto, sonata, symphony, etc.) you get not a musical re-creation of actual human experience or emotion (you do get this in "program" music—*Til Eulenspiegel*, or *Der Erlkönig*, or *The Sorcerer's Apprentice*), but a case in point, under the species of tone and interval and sequence, of structure and harmony (even if that is suggested by contrast: we still hear *dis*sonance as dissonance, and syncopation as syncopation—it has nothing to do with what we prefer; it exists in relation to some prior idea of harmony and rhythm with which we begin). By the same token, the power of Dante or Milton appears in the extent to which he can take the stuff of our experience (guilt, evil, joy, etc.), and give it such shape that we find our awareness of our own experience suddenly heightened. That, of course, is what it is all about—all this drama and music and poetry: it is the human way of taking a look at its own experience, and of uttering something about that experience. It is not that experience, although it does, if we let it, give that experience back to us, sharpened and focused and burnished.

But we are not all Verdis and Miltons. Nor can we all spend every evening at the theater. And we can thank heaven for that. For the business of life is not so much to observe experience (although that is close to the center) as to participate in experience. And presumably one is human to the extent that he participates authentically in those experiences that specially characterize human existence (as opposed to angelic or avian or simian existence). Whatever else a man (king or serf) may be doing, there are various things which mark his experience, and the viewpoint being put here is that it is those universals which lie at the center of significance, and that the variables (whether he gets to move in court circles, climb the Himalayas, write epic poetry, or mix sundaes) are just that—variables. They may color and shape his experience, but they do not determine its essence. The king and the serf must both be born in precisely the same way, and must learn to walk and talk, and must eat periodically, and sleep, and learn that one *may* do this and may *not* do that; and grow up, putting away the toys and taking up the scepter or plow; and marry (probably), with all the potential which that holds for exploring the nature of love; and must go on day after day and year after year, doing what is required; and must grow feeble and infirm and then die. And it is the supposition here that these commonplaces—these given rhythms of experience—constitute the imagery under which we may all participate in the way things are. And, corollary to this, that the failure to seize these humdrum commonplaces as vitally significant, or the effort to fly from them and seek fulfillment in various forms of substitution or diversion, represents a misapprehension of what it means to be authentically human.

This view, carried to the *n*th place, would go like this, then: things are not random; they are, finally, glorious, and the diagram of this glory appears everywhere and on all levels—in astronomy and in zoology and botany and anatomy and oceanography—and is enacted by man in his politics and institutions, and acknowledged and celebrated in his rituals and his art. And it is configured most immediately and obviously for him in the commonplaces of his life. So that, working from the bottom up, he might see those commonplaces as images of that ultimate glory, and find in them clues as to the nature of that glory.

Hence, when he observes in his own experience that a child issues from the union of the man and the woman, he might suspect that it is in the nature of union to produce fruit, or, conversely, that the fruit owes its life to a prior union. Further, he might observe that it is in the nature of that union to be ecstatic, and he might thus conclude that joy is somehow written into the sources of life. And he will undoubtedly see that there are pain and agony involved and will have to come to terms with what he can see only as an intrusion or an ambiguity—that pain is somehow bound up in the whole process of joy. And, seeing his infant suck its mother's breasts, he will understand that growth and strength derive from nourishment, and that that nourishment issues from the self-giving of another life—milk from the mother, or meat from the calf, or flour from the wheat. And he might see that all these humdrum necessities—dishes and laundry and cooking—are the accouterments to the liturgies celebrated in this temple.

Moreover, watching that growth, he will see the paradox that authentic freedom is won not by the child's being granted every wish (an infinite number of chocolates, dancing on the windowsill, etc.), but rather by curbing and channeling and, alas, denying. And in the denial (and perhaps punishment) he will observe again that there is a lamentable discrepancy at work in things, tearing at the fabric of the diagram—in this case a discrepancy between inclination (more chocolates) and perfection (good teeth). He will see also that the truth of the matter is not necessarily known intuitively by the growing child, but that facts have to be *learned*, either by authority (thou shalt not put thy pinkie in that gas flame) or by experience (ouch). And he will see at work over a long, long span of time the difficult notion that reward or fulfillment commonly follows rigor and renunciation and austerity (the winning pole vault, the Ph.D.), and is not available on demand.

And in his own experience he may observe that his greatest liberty occurs (he can only see this in retrospect, since it vanishes the moment it is looked at) when he is least conscious of himself—when he is hard at work on some piece of research, focusing on the data, or when he is carried away upon hearing an aria sung by Birgit Nilsson, or when he is loving his wife, either passionately or in some simple act like bringing breakfast to her in bed. It will occur to him that one of the oddities of love (erotic, paternal, filial, social) is that its motion is outward and away from itself, and that it experiences this motion as joy: and, conversely, he may discover if he visits his psychiatrist often enough that there is an unsettling ratio between a person's unhappiness and his concentration on himself.

And so on: on and on, until he shuffles, through debility and hebetude, toward that final horror that seems to settle it once and forever that there is discrepancy at work in things—this time the discrepancy between our dreams of destiny and our actual experience of dissolution—and that the Conqueror Worm has the last word.

But he might note, because he has looked around him at a thousand images, that it is not unobserved that life issues from death—that spring rises from winter, and the oak from the dead acorn, and dawn from the night, and Phoenix from the ashes.

These are all old moral saws. Nothing new here. Bromides. But then there is nothing new anywhere. The business of the poet and prophet has always been to take the saws and astonish and delight us into a fresh awareness of what they mean by discovering them suddenly in this image, and in this, and this. And the rest of us may see it all either as a pointless jumble of phenomena, or as the diagram of glory—as grinding tediously toward entropy, or as dancing toward the Dance.